Escapes from Cayenne

Escapes from Cayenne

A STORY OF SOCIALISM
AND SLAVERY IN AN AGE OF
REVOLUTION AND REACTION

Léon Chautard

EDITED AND
WITH AN INTRODUCTION
BY MICHAËL ROY

The University of Georgia Press
ATHENS

Most University of Georgia Press titles are
available from popular e-book vendors.

Printed digitally

Library of Congress Control Number: 2023002879
ISBN: 9780820365886 (hardback)
ISBN: 9780820364803 (paperback)
ISBN: 9780820364810 (epub)
ISBN: 9780820364827 (PDF)

CONTENTS

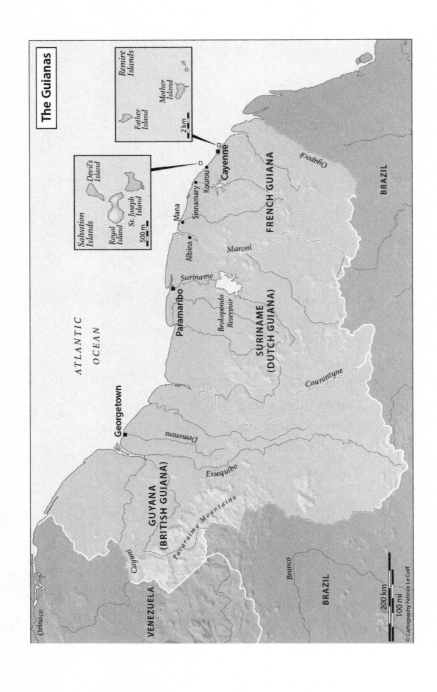

Escapes from Cayenne

EDITOR'S INTRODUCTION

Michaël Roy

Translated by Thomas C. Jones

> And who are in the prisons, in the fortresses, in the cells, . . . at
> Cayenne, and in exile? Law, honor, intelligence, liberty, and right.
>
> —VICTOR HUGO, *Napoleon the Little* (1852)

The nineteenth century has been described by one French historian as "the century of exiles."[1] The failed French revolution of 1848 in particular forced a number of republican political and literary figures into exile in cities like London, Brussels, Geneva, and New York, as well as in more isolated locations like the small island of Jersey in the English Channel. The celebrated novelist, poet, and playwright Victor Hugo was perhaps the most famous of these *proscrits*, as they came to be called. Some of his most important works, including his masterpiece *Les Misérables* (1862), were written during his fifteen-year exile on the Channel Island of Guernsey.

Meanwhile, thousands of far less well-known individuals—insurgent workers, opponents of Louis-Napoleon Bonaparte's coup of December 2, 1851, heads of republican secret societies—were transported to overseas *bagnes* (prisons) in Algeria and French Guiana. This book attempts to retrieve one of these figures, the socialist Léon Chautard (1812–1890), from this comparative obscurity. Because the deportation of French political prisoners (and common-law criminals) was undertaken on a large scale in the 1850s, it has more often been approached by historians as a collective experience than as an individual one. The revolution of 1848 itself is generally treated through the use of statistics rather than biogra-

phy, and most of the workers who revolted during the Parisian insurrection of June 1848 (*les journées de juin*, or June Days) remain unknown to
us.[2] This makes it difficult to answer several crucial questions. What was
daily life like for those who were transported and subjected to hard labor
in faraway colonies? How did this experience transform those who survived it? Some personal accounts were published at the time, for instance
that of the journalist and future Communard Charles Delescluze, who
was sent to Guiana in 1858, shortly before a general amnesty was proclaimed in August 1859, and whose memoirs appeared in Paris in 1869
under the title *From Paris to Cayenne*.[3] Chautard's own autobiographical account of his life as a political prisoner and a transportee, *Escapes
from Cayenne* (1857), was written in English and published in the United
States, where Chautard lived for fifteen years. There was no French edition of this work, and it has long been forgotten by U.S. readers.

A scholar of early African American print culture and the U.S. abolition movement, I first came across Chautard in the correspondence of the
white abolitionist William Lloyd Garrison while working on a book on the
publication, circulation, and reception of antebellum slave narratives.[4] In
a letter to an unknown correspondent in February 1858, Garrison shared
his "very deep interest" in the case of three "French refugees from the
despotism of L[ouis] N[apoleon]" who had recently arrived in Massachusetts. One of them, "Mr. C.," had published "the thrilling N[arrative]
of their escape from C[ayenne]," of which Garrison attached twenty-five
copies.[5] I was struck by the parallels between these refugees and the formerly enslaved men and women whose writings I was then investigating.
Though the experiences of their lives had been wholly incomparable up
to then, both had escaped from forms of imprisonment and found assistance among northern abolitionists, and both had felt the need to write
and publish accounts of these trials. Moreover, Garrison explained that
the three French refugees were thoroughly antislavery. I was intrigued by
this unlikely encounter between French revolutionary republicanism and
U.S. abolitionism on the eve of the Civil War and decided that I would
have to know more. Several years passed before I finally took the time to
read *Escapes from Cayenne*.

Originally published in Salem, Massachusetts, as a sixty-three-page
pamphlet, *Escapes from Cayenne* is as much about Chautard's two political companions, Hippolyte Paon and Charles Bivors, as it is about Chautard himself. The text can be confusing on first reading. The chronology

of events is not always clear, there are frequent digressions, and navigating the contemporary lexicon can be tricky. The central third of the book consists of a separate, embedded narrative: Chautard reproduces lengthy extracts from his friend Paon's journal, which he translates from French into English. In contrast to Delescluze's account, a work that was patiently composed and carefully edited by a professional writer, *Escapes from Cayenne* is a messy, polyphonic document written in haste by someone who was not a native speaker of English and who barely had time to recover from his decade-long ordeal. Still, Chautard's narrative remains a riveting read. It is a thrilling tale of adventure, replete with twists and turns, tracing a course strewn with obstacles and danger, from the barricades of Paris to the forests of Guiana and on to the streets of Boston. It is an autobiography told in the singular voice of a man ready to sacrifice all to defend his cause—a man who never loses his sense of humor, however, even in the most perilous situations. Finally, it is a political manifesto, one that advocates the overthrow of all forms of oppression and exploitation—capitalism, slavery, imperialism—and the creation of a new, more egalitarian society.

Escapes from Cayenne covers only one part of Chautard's life, from the February Days of 1848 until his arrival in the United States in September 1857. In this introduction I draw from both French and U.S. archival sources to reconstruct his life before and after this crucial decade. I pay particular attention to how his commitment to justice and equality developed over time, especially as a result of his experience as a transportee and then as an exile in the United States. Chautard's transatlantic trajectory sheds light on the international ramifications of the revolution of 1848 at a time when nineteenth-century French historians are calling for a move away from a purely European perspective to better appreciate what a recently published volume calls the "worlds of 1848." Likewise, this book contributes to the ongoing transnational turn in the history of the early United States.[6] Through their movements, both coerced and voluntary, Chautard, his two companions, and the republicans they met on their way helped to make the revolution a global event and connect it to antislavery struggles in the Americas.

From Southern France to Montmartre

Jean Léon Ricard Chautard was born on December 1, 1812, in Gallargues, a village located halfway between Nîmes and Montpellier, not far from the Mediterranean coast. His parents, Michel Chautard and Marie Ricard, both natives of the region, had been married for over a decade, and Léon was likely not their first child. Their marriage certificate provides information regarding the family's professional background. Both of Léon's grandfathers were farmers; his father distilled brandy.[7] Two of his maternal uncles, we learn in *Escapes from Cayenne*, fought as officers—and died—in Napoleon's ill-fated Russian campaign, which ended in the winter of 1812, around the time of Léon's birth. Two years later, Lieutenant Jean-François Chautard ferried back the exiled emperor from Elba to France, facilitating his (failed) return to power. As a republican, Léon Chautard was not particularly proud of his family's loyalty to Napoleon. In his narrative, he explains how, before his departure for Cayenne in September 1852, a police officer encouraged him to ask Louis-Napoleon for a pardon, promising that the prince-president (Louis-Napoleon's title at the time) knew who he was and would show him clemency. Faithful to his political convictions, Chautard refused to beg for a pardon from the man whom he variously calls in his pamphlet "the crowned Sycophant," "Bonaparte, the perfidious," or the "poor dwarf"—epithets that echo those hurled by Victor Hugo at "Napoleon the Little" in his volume of the same name.[8]

Yet the young Chautard did in fact briefly consider following in his uncles' footsteps. At the age of eighteen, he enlisted in the 6th Line Infantry Regiment, where he was rapidly promoted to corporal. A late (and unreliable) source claims that he fought in Algeria, which France invaded in 1830 and annexed four years later.[9] But Chautard was already showing himself to be resistant to authority. He was demoted "for misconduct" in May 1834, designated a deserter in August 1835, and "struck off for prolonged absence" in March 1837. Having reappeared in November 1838, he was finally dismissed from the army without a trial.[10] Doubtless this military experience, irregular though it was, proved useful to him later on the Parisian barricades in 1848 and during the U.S. Civil War. The four years he spent traveling through England, likely between 1838 and 1842, were likewise formative. Not only did Chautard learn English during this time, but he may also have been in contact with the ideas of the socialist thinker Robert Owen and perhaps witnessed the emergence of the Chartist movement.

By 1848 Chautard had settled in Paris, or more precisely, in the neighboring independent commune of Montmartre, "one of the principal revolutionary islets in the popular Parisian archipelago."[11] He lived there with his wife Clémentine Chautard (née Collare), originally from Valenciennes, a city in northern France. In *Escapes from Cayenne* he recalls "my black eyed and black haired lady, whose love and devotion bore up my fainting courage, in many circumstances, and made my happiness for many years!" The quarter of a century that Léon and Clémentine spent away from each other did nothing to erode the strength of their bond, and they were reunited after Léon returned from his U.S. exile in 1872.

Chautard, who had received a solid education, worked as a bookkeeper for various Parisian merchants, including Pierron, in the Rue Saint-Honoré, and the Angrémy brothers, wholesalers in "merino, shawls, and novelties."[12] His employers did not hesitate to testify in his favor after he was arrested. In October 1848 Pierron attested: "I declare that the named . . . Chautard has been employed for several years in my establishment as a cashier. And I can vouch for him, as a friend, being intimately associated with him for sixteen years. I can also state, knowing the righteousness of his sentiments, that his public and private conduct has never failed to be honorable so long as I have known him." The Angrémy brothers further testified that Chautard had always "conducted himself as a man of honor."[13]

Politically, Chautard was a fervent republican and socialist and a passionate defender of *la République démocratique et sociale*. For him, republicanism meant more than a mere transformation of political institutions; the change of regime brought about by the February Days and the formation of a provisional republican government was only the first step toward the realization of a larger, more ambitious *social* project. The essence of socialism, as he put it in his narrative, was "to seek the best means of securing to all citizens of the commonwealth the greatest portion of comfort, knowledge, freedom—of *happiness*, in one word." Chautard was a "romantic socialist," to use Jonathan Beecher's term. His ideal society was "bound by ties of love and affection" and "based on cooperation rather than competition, on solidarity rather than egoism."[14] As

Samuel Hayat has shown, two conceptions of republicanism vied against each other in the months between February and June. One was concerned with order and moderation, the other with emancipation and collective welfare. Of these two antagonistic understandings of what *la République* entailed, the first eventually prevailed—until a self-appointed, autocratic emperor crushed the Second Republic itself.[15]

On the Barricades

One can easily imagine how euphoric Chautard must have felt during those few months when *la République démocratique et sociale* still seemed attainable. Even before legislation affirming the rights to assembly and association was passed, hundreds of political clubs were formed, both in Paris and across France. People met in cafés and at public halls to discuss new ideas and, within the most radical groups at least, invent a new world. "Nothing contributed so powerfully to the initiation of the people into democratic life as the clubs," the republican Louis Ménard declared in 1849.[16] Chautard hoped to play a prominent part in this revolutionary process and, even as his presidency of one of these clubs was challenged by other members, he confided to a fellow socialist that he had aspired to be a "possible man" of the revolution—a curious but evocative choice of term. During the revolutionary *journées* of 1848, the political terrain shifted too rapidly for any such position to be permanently viable, though this did nothing to lessen his determination. Chautard was, in his own words, a "man of the head and of the heart" who had "dedicated his existence to the holy cause of humanity."[17]

Chautard was involved in the Club Républicain de Montmartre, the Club Républicain, the Club des Montagnards, and the Club de la Révolution Démocratique. Alphonse Lucas, a critical observer of the revolution, used the same adjective to describe the first three of these clubs— "red." This was the color of the banner with which the Parisian workers had hoped to replace the tricolor in February 1848, though Alphonse de Lamartine, a celebrated writer and prominent member of the new republic's provisional government, was ultimately successful in winning their support back over to the old flag. The fourth of these clubs was just as "red" in its declaration of principles, addressed to the workers and signed by Chautard, demanding "the abolition of all privileges in any form what-

"The burning of the throne." Bibliothèque nationale de France.

soever, of the exploitation of man by man, of social distinctions, . . . and generally of everything that violates the sacred principle of equality."[18] Chautard also contributed to some of the newspapers that proliferated alongside the democratic clubs. Yet it was in the National Workshops that he took his most radical actions. Created by the provisional government at the end of February, these were public-works projects intended to provide employment to Paris's workers in the aftermath of the recent economic crisis. The National Workshops were but a pale copy of the "social workshops"—workers' cooperative factories—proposed by the socialist Louis Blanc; they in fact bore a greater resemblance to the charitable institutions of the Ancien Régime. Furthermore, the indigent came to the workshops in numbers too large for all to be employed. Conceived as a means of calming popular revolutionary fervor, the workshops became instead a venue for the diffusion of socialist ideas. Chautard was in contact with the National Workshops, where he engaged, in the words of a prefect of police, in "an active propaganda in favor of demagogic ideas."[19] The closure of the workshops, approved on June 21 by the majority of moderate republicans in the constituent national assembly, triggered the June uprising. "It was well known," Ménard commented, "that the dissolution of the National Workshops, by simultaneously condemning one hundred thousand men to die of hunger, would ignite a civil war."[20]

What role did Chautard play in the June Days? The dossier of the military commission of inquiry on the insurrection gives contradictory accounts. Interrogated by a police officer after his arrest, Chautard denied having taken part in the fighting, admitting only that he had been in the area of the Faubourg Poissonnière, where several barricades had been erected. To the question "What were you doing on the Poissonnière barricades on June 24?" he simply responded, "I wanted to see what was going on." "You have been seen leading a barricade or rather commanding insurgents," the officer insisted. "That's not true," Chautard retorted, without further comment. The accusations of the commission of inquiry relied in large part on the testimony of Denis-Étienne Collas, an assistant to the mayor of Montmartre, who had been responsible for the closure of the Club Républicain de Montmartre the previous month. Collas claimed to have seen Chautard first on the morning of June 23, in the Rue des Martyrs, when Chautard and two men accompanying him "had been urging the workers of the National Workshops to leave, which they did en masse." Their exchange was turbulent, with Chautard asking Collas, "Are you going to send down your bulldogs today?" Collas claimed to have seen Chautard again the next evening, in the Faubourg Poissonnière, where a thousand men held an impregnable barricade. In a single sentence, he sealed the fate of Chautard: "He seemed to me to be the leader of the barricade."[21] Whether accurate or not, this account was the one recorded by the authorities. According to the prefect of police cited above, Chautard not only "commanded the barrier of the Faubourg Poissonnière" during the insurrection of June, but he "exercised a great influence over the insurgents who fought under his orders."[22]

The four-day battle ended with the defeat of the insurgents and their bloody repression by General Eugène Cavaignac. Over a thousand insurgents died on the barricades and several thousand more, including Chautard, were arrested during and after the uprising.[23] While a significant number were eventually released, Chautard was taken from prison to prison in Paris and then in Le Havre and Brest, where he was held on the floating jails known as pontoons. Back in Paris, his wife Clémentine pleaded his innocence in a letter dated January 12, 1849, and addressed to Louis-Napoleon, who had just been elected president of the new republic:

> Monsieur le Président,
>
> Léon Ricard Chautard, bookkeeper, my husband, arrested following calumnious denunciations on July 9 last year and imprisoned since that date, finds himself today an inmate on board the pontoon *Uranie*, in the harbor of Brest.
>
> Having only my husband's labor for sustenance, I was forced, after having given up the little furniture that I possessed, to accept the hospitality of a family member living in the countryside.
>
> Before I leave the capital allow an unfortunate woman to reach out to you, Monsieur le Président, so that my husband might be set at liberty—a liberty of which he should never have been deprived.
>
> The numerous and honorable certificates, delivered by respectable personages who have known my husband for many years, and which have been sent to the clemency commission, will convince you, Monsieur le Président, of his innocence, and of the part your benevolence can play in relieving his sufferings.[24]

Nothing came of this. Chautard remained incarcerated.

"The floating prison." Maurice Alhoy, *Les Bagnes: Histoire, types, mœurs, mystères* (1845). École nationale d'administration pénitentiaire / Centre de ressources sur l'histoire des crimes et des peines.

Chautard spent most of the year 1849 in Belle-Île-en-Mer (or "Belle Isle," as he writes in his narrative), an island off the coast of Brittany where a prison had been established following the June uprising. This facility, which rapidly became a major detention center for republicans and socialists, saw the rebirth of a form of democratic life through club meetings and the emergence of makeshift newspapers. With two of his fellow detainees, Chautard made the first of many attempted escapes, as he recounts in *Escapes from Cayenne*, and as is confirmed by another transportee, Jean-Baptiste Dunaud, in his own account.[25] The administrators of Belle-Île were particularly suspicious of Chautard. Written in the prison's records, next to his name, is found "Firebrand, man of action. Dangerous in all respects. Ardent ringleader, very bad." Hippolyte Paon, who also passed through Belle-Île, aroused the same fears: "Redoubtable, capable of all kinds of violence."[26] The nervousness of the administration reached its peak on December 11 and 12, 1849. An altercation between the prisoners and guards got out of hand, with one detainee killed and ten others then put on trial. Chautard and several of his companions were accused of having provoked a prisoners' rebellion.[27] Although he was acquitted, Chautard learned after the trial that he was to be transported to Algeria.

Colonial Punishments

The deportation of political dissidents was initiated soon after the June insurrection. A decree issued on June 27 stipulated that "individuals currently detained who are known to have taken part in the insurrection beginning on June 23" will be "transported, for national security, to overseas colonies." A law of January 24, 1850, specified where the prisoners would be sent: "All individuals currently detained at Belle-Île, who have been condemned to transportation by the decree of June 27, 1848, . . . will be transferred to Algeria." The initial decree anticipated mass transportation, but because of the number of pardons subsequently issued, the law of 1850 only dealt with fewer than five hundred insurgents.[28] In a letter to his mother written shortly after his arrival in Algeria, Dunaud commented on these measures in language that could have come from the hand of Chautard:

> By this decree is reaction ridding itself of the nightmare which haunts it? Does it believe that, because we are condemned without trial, it

has shielded itself from socialism?—No.—Today socialism is a giant which can no longer be torn down. . . . It is this which should give us happiness, which should take away all of our future worries and which will destroy the tyrannical oppression of the rich which has filled our lives with venom and bitterness. Therefore, I regard this persecution as a gift from providence, because it is only this which can clarify the sacred precepts of socialism and increase the already innumerable army of believers in the new religion, which I consider to be universal, because it will destroy the servitude which weighs down all the peoples and will convert the world into one vast republic.[29]

Deporting political opponents to distant territories became a regular practice for the French government in the 1850s. As many as ten thousand were sent to Algeria and French Guiana during the Second Republic and Second Empire.

Chautard spent a little over two years in Algeria, where once again he was taken from one prison to another. He was first interned in the casbah of Bône—large fortified barracks nestled in the heights of the city (known today as Annaba)—then sent to Algiers, Oran, and Mers el-Kébir. In all of these places political prisoners were subjected to poor treatment and severe discipline. "We were starving and slowly dying," Chautard writes in *Escapes from Cayenne*. "The most trivial infraction was often punished with three, four, or five days in solitary confinement," adds Delescluze in *From Paris to Cayenne*.[30] Repression in France was ratcheted up again after Louis-Napoleon's December 1851 coup. So-called "mixed commissions" condemned suspects in expedited proceedings. Guiana, where the French had had a foothold since the seventeenth century and where several hundred refractory priests were transported during the French Revolution, now seemed like an appropriate destination for those prisoners—political and common-law alike—that the regime wanted to keep as far away from the metropole as possible. Multiple decrees were issued to that effect, with that of May 31, 1852, stating: "The transportees of 1848 who, since their arrival in Algeria have received . . . punishment for insubordination or any other crime, will be taken to Cayenne." The indomitable Chautard had twice been condemned to five years in irons for insulting his "superiors," on June 4, 1851, and June 10, 1852. In September 1852, he became the first of the June insurgents to be transported to Guiana, a lone political prisoner among the common-law criminals who had

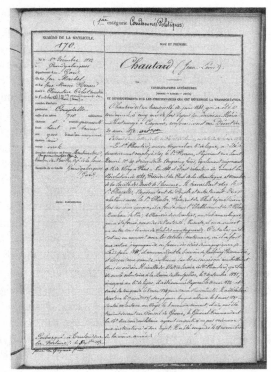

Léon Chautard's personal file. Archives nationales d'outre-mer.

in the past several months been collected from the metropolitan *bagnes* to be sent to the other side of the Atlantic. Paon and Bivors followed in July 1853. Thirty of the June insurgents would eventually be transported to Cayenne.

Escapes from Cayenne sheds light on the ordeals endured by the *transportés* in the early days of the penal colony. Chautard, Paon, and Bivors spent long, miserable months on the three small islands off the coast of Guiana known as the Salvation Islands—St. Joseph Island, Royal Island, and the notorious Devil's Island. "We were covered with chains," Chautard writes. "We worked the whole day under a tropical sun. . . . We stayed at St. Joseph Island for nineteen months, and lost fifty of our companions—the fourth of us. They died from despair, want of food, ill treatment, and dysentery." In his own narrative, Paon recounts an instance of torture on the pillory which, as primitive as it seems, is corroborated by other accounts. *Escapes from Cayenne* does not differ significantly from

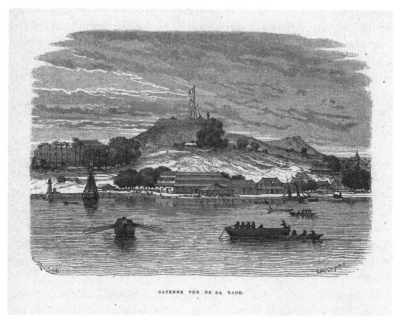

"Cayenne seen from the harbor." Frédéric Bouyer, *La Guyane française:
Notes et souvenirs d'un voyage exécuté en 1862–1863* (1867). Bibliothèque
numérique Manioc / Collection privée Philippe Batrosse.

other transportation narratives: hard labor, punishment, and disease con-
sumed the daily lives of the prisoners. Chautard's lot was comparatively
better than that of many of his companions. Of his five years in Guiana,
he spent half in the city of Cayenne, where he enjoyed a limited amount
of freedom. His expertise in accounting made him more useful to the
creation of the Bank of Guiana in 1855 than to excavation work and the
construction of barracks on the islands. Paon and Bivors, for their part,
seem to have spent most of their three years of captivity on the Salvation
Islands.

In this hostile environment, prisoners forged brotherly bonds that
made life more bearable. Delescluze wrote of the friendships that he made
in Belle-Île "in the sacred fraternity of misfortune," while another transportee, Jacques-Eugène Leiris, dedicated several moving passages of his
correspondence to his evenings spent walking in the courtyard of the casbah of Bône "with three friends, . . . three brave souls." "We were insep-

arable," he added, "and often we were able to spend several happy hours sharing our confidences and our hopes."[31] Though such moments of respite were less common in Guiana, this did not prevent Chautard, Paon, and Bivors—three "brave souls" themselves—from becoming closer over time. Their friendship was political, cemented by the desire for a better and fairer world. Their reunion in Demerara, on British soil, after escaping Guiana, resembles the scenes portrayed in Leiris's letter: "After supper we took a walk, Paon on one side, Bivors on the other, and I in the middle. We talked about our captivity, our friends, our hopes and our escape." Certainly, there were some tensions among the transportees, as Chautard suggests in his passages on Algeria. These men did not necessarily share the same political opinions, and they did not all come from the same social backgrounds. They formed a very human community, which, like any other, included inevitable dissension and conflict. But in *Escapes from Cayenne*, Paon and Chautard linger less on conflict and more on the fraternal links and the spirit of solidarity that made their escape possible.

Because he resided in Cayenne, Chautard was able, after several attempts, to secretly board a ship embarking for British Guiana on July 14, 1857. Apparently, he was not informed that the plea for clemency that he had sent to the emperor a few months before was successful; he would have been released on October 2.[32] Meanwhile, Paon and Bivors escaped with thirty-two other prisoners on two rafts that they managed to construct. This was nothing short of a miracle, since the Salvation Islands essentially constituted an open-air prison that was nearly impossible to escape, let alone for prisoners in a state of physical and moral exhaustion. The *bagne*'s administration, counting on "the material impossibility of a flight," did not take the trouble to closely monitor the transportees.[33] Chautard transcribed Paon's journal of his flight into *Escapes from Cayenne*, and its depictions of hurricanes, quicksand, and flesh-eating crabs illustrate the fugitives' hardships in a striking manner. Paon's journal, however, is interesting not only for its thrilling incidents, but also for what it shows of an Atlantic civilization fashioned by three centuries of migrations, circulation, and exchange. On their travels from French to Dutch to British Guiana, the fugitives encounter a composite population of Indigenous men and women, Maroons, Dutch colonists, and Portuguese sailors—some of whom bar their route, while others give them assistance. Notably, Paon and Bivors find an ally in the German explorer

"An Indian village." Pierre-Jacques Benoît, *Voyage à Surinam:*
Description des possessions néerlandaises dans la Guyane (1839).
Bibliothèque numérique Manioc / Archives territoriales de Guyane.

"A fugitive slave." Pierre-Jacques Benoît, *Voyage à Surinam:*
Description des possessions néerlandaises dans la Guyane (1839).
Bibliothèque numérique Manioc / Archives territoriales de Guyane.

and naturalist August Kappler, who in 1846 had founded the settlement of Albina on the Maroni River, at the border between French Guiana and Suriname (Dutch Guiana). There they discover a small multiethnic and interracial community where Black men and women work freely. His passage through Albina gives Paon the occasion to develop a critique of slavery that forms a key aspect of his and Chautard's political thinking.

Slavery, Abolition, and the Revolution of 1848

Slavery is denounced forcefully and repeatedly in *Escapes from Cayenne*. French colonial slavery had been abolished in 1794, following the slave insurrection of Saint-Domingue (Haiti), only to be reestablished by Napoleon in 1802. It was abolished again, this time permanently, in the wake of the revolution of 1848. Slavery was "an attack against human dignity," the emancipation decree of April 27, 1848, stated, "a flagrant violation of the republican values of Liberty, Equality, and Fraternity." It was to be abolished "in all French colonies and possessions" two months later. In fact, several slave revolts precipitated the application of the decree, as happened in Martinique, where the insurrection of May 22 led to an accelerated abolition on the following day. France's abolition of slavery in 1848 is mentioned in Paon's narrative when two unidentified Black men, likely former slaves, come to the rescue of the fugitives as they find themselves in a dangerous impasse with a group of Indians: "You fought in the year 1848, for the abolition of slavery, and you co-operated to the downfall of that degrading institution," one of them says to the runaway republicans. "You are in safety here; you are as safe as in your own homes."

Paon's and Chautard's radical critique of slavery sheds light on a popular, grassroots brand of abolitionism that has long been neglected by historians. French abolitionism is often presented as a Paris-centered political movement, one organized from 1834 by a small, elitist body, the French Society for the Abolition of Slavery, which focused on so-called amelioration policies and advocated gradual (rather than immediate) emancipation. Recent syntheses pay little attention to slave resistance and to the activism of free people of color, women, and white workers, except for that of a few figures such as the writer Germaine de Staël or the Black abolitionist Cyrille Bissette.[34] Workers in the metropole did not remain silent on the question of slavery: several workers' petitions were sent to the Chamber of Deputies in 1844, some of which must have been signed by future insurgents of 1848. "It is to obey the great principle of human fraternity," one petition stated, "that we come to plead the cause of our unfortunate brothers, the slaves."[35] The workers' argument was mostly couched in humanitarian terms and based on egalitarian principles. It took a more radical turn when coupled, as in Paon's narrative, with an attack on the rich and powerful:

> Slaveholders confine us for want of money, slavery having no other right than force and no other purpose than money making. Slaveholders, you are men of money; you would do everything for money, and it is very lucky indeed that the sun is so far from your crooked hands and so difficult to catch; otherwise you would take it, saying that God made it for you alone, as you are not ashamed to say that God permits slavery; you would take the sun, share it amongst you, put your part in your deepest pockets, and we, poor disgraced men, would be obliged to stay in eternal darkness, or to purchase light of you.

Socialism, Paon and Chautard argued, must fight slavery as a system based on racial oppression but also as a system of capitalist accumulation, by which a minority of speculators enriched themselves at the expense of the majority. The "proletarian worker of Europe" and "the proletarian slave of the colonies," to borrow from the Martinican intellectual Aimé Césaire, shared a common enemy—capitalism—whose emergence in the nineteenth century relied on the joint exploitation of both.[36] An extreme form of the exploitation of man by man, slavery must be actively opposed by socialists.

Paon's and Chautard's abolitionism also drew on their own experience of deportation and forced labor. It was not a coincidence that the establishment of a penal colony in Guiana followed hard on the heels of abolition. The transportation of prisoners to Cayenne was partly devised as a substitute for slavery. It allowed not only the banishment of undesirable elements and the emptying of overcrowded metropolitan prisons but also the replacement of the emancipated Black workforce in the colonies. Louis Eugène Gaultier de La Richerie, a colonial administrator mentioned several times in *Escapes from Cayenne*, put it succinctly: "These damned republicans have . . . [abolished] slavery in the colonies; they will replace the blacks."[37] The harsh treatment meted out to the prisoners sometimes resembled that previously inflicted on the enslaved. Paon's graphic account of torture on the pillory is reminiscent of scenes of violence commonly found in English-language slave narratives, while the political prisoner François Attibert's description of the living conditions on board the ship taking him across the Atlantic brings to mind the infamous Middle Passage: "Everyone will understand how twenty-seven men in such a cramped space, seasick, exhausted by the time they spent in prison, lacking air and food, may suffer." Dunaud went so far as to write that the transported prisoners were "piled up like negroes in the hold of a slave ship."[38] Ultimately, it was the feeling of "being treated like a slave" that prompted Chautard to run away from Cayenne.

This temporary experience of coercion and violence made these political prisoners all the more sympathetic to the plight of the enslaved in the Americas. Several events recounted in *Escapes from Cayenne* reinforced Paon's and Chautard's antislavery convictions. While in Cayenne, Chautard was imprisoned "for two months for having called '*Slave Dealer*' a man who was, in fact, a retailer of negroes" (possibly a Dutch trader in transit, as the Dutch did not abolish slavery in their colonies until 1863). During their time in Albina, Paon and Bivors met the chief of one of the Maroon peoples of Suriname—descendants of enslaved Africans who had escaped from plantations in the seventeenth and eighteenth centuries and formed settlements in the interior rainforests. In the manner of an ethnographer, Paon devotes several paragraphs of his narrative to the history and culture of the Maroons, whose capacity for resistance and autonomy he clearly admires.[39] In his autobiography, Attibert explains how Black freedmen and white workers support each other in Cayenne, with the former helping the latter to escape:

> When the negroes, engaged in free employment, are called upon to demonstrate skills, they show themselves to be just as ingenious as European workers. . . . They are adroit and courageous sailors, tireless on foot and as porters. . . . Their political ideas are, for the most part, excellent. The revolution of 1848 did them much good. At Cayenne, the political deportees are loved by them. They understand that the cause for which we fight is a universal cause.[40]

For their part, Attibert and his fellow fugitives protest against the whipping of enslaved people in Paramaribo, the capital of Suriname. "This punishment enraged us to the point that we momentarily forgot our own misfortune and wrote the governor a letter in which we claimed human

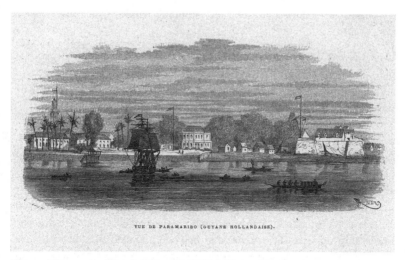

VUE DE PARAMARIBO (GUYANE HOLLANDAISE).

"View of Paramaribo (Dutch Guiana)." Frédéric Bouyer, *La Guyane française: Notes et souvenirs d'un voyage exécuté en 1862-1863* (1867). Bibliothèque numérique Manioc / Collection privée Philippe Batrosse.

rights for the blacks."[41] A number of these French fugitives eventually reached the United States, where they also agitated against slavery.

French Socialists Come to the United States

No sooner did Chautard set foot in Guiana than he contemplated running away to the United States, a country that he thought of as the embodiment of democracy. Echoes of Tocqueville can be heard in *Escapes of Cayenne*, as when Chautard writes that "people [in the United States] elect their magistrates, from the President of the Republic to the modest town selectmen. Having the right to elect them, they have the right to dismiss them when they act wrong." Chautard was also aware that the United States had long been a land of refuge for European immigrants:

> There, perhaps people will remember that their ancestors of Massachusetts and Pennsylvania were poor pilgrims as we are; that they were exiled Puritans and exiled Quakers, who had fled from persecutors and persecutions in England and Germany. Those models of freedom will, perhaps, admit us in their Commonwealth; they will give us an asy-

lum, protection, friendship, and honorable employment. This is all we want.

Escapes from Cayenne ends with a panegyric to the "country of Washington"—a "promised land" where Chautard, Paon, and Bivors hope to finally live in peace and to continue defending their ideas without fear of repression.

Chautard's slightly forced lyricism in the final paragraphs of his narrative can also be read as a strategy to ingratiate himself with a U.S. public on whose financial and material assistance he depended. For Chautard was likely aware that the United States was anything but a "land of liberty" in 1857. Although slavery had long been abolished in the North, it thrived in the Deep South and kept extending westward as the national domain grew in size and the domestic slave trade intensified. Recent scholarship on U.S. slavery, or what has been labeled the New History of Capitalism, has characterized the production of slave-grown cotton as a catalyst to America's economic growth. The industrialization of the North, historians show, went hand in hand with the expansion of slavery in the South. Southern cotton fed the northern textile industry and was also exported to European countries such as Great Britain and France. Profits derived from cotton boosted the national (as well as international) economy, flowing from the plantations of Louisiana to the mills of New England via the banks and insurance companies of New York.[42]

The practice of slavery and the support it received from the federal government aroused fierce opposition in civil society. African Americans and a growing number of white men and women campaigned against what they denounced as a dehumanizing system that flouted basic republican principles of liberty and equality. After a first period of antislavery agitation following the American Revolution, the 1830s saw the rise of a second abolitionist wave, led by activists who demanded the immediate end of slavery and hoped to transform America into an interracial democracy. William Lloyd Garrison, who in 1831 founded the antislavery newspaper *The Liberator*, and the Black writer and orator Frederick Douglass were two of the best-known figures of this emerging social movement. For the most radical of the abolitionists, the fight against slavery and racial proscription was part of a larger struggle against all forms of oppression in the United States and abroad. These activists also advocated for women's rights, organized against Indian Removal, and drew attention to the poor

William Lloyd Garrison, c. 1860. Collection of the Smithsonian National Museum of African American History and Culture, Gift of the Garrison Family in memory of George Thompson Garrison.

Frederick Douglass, c. 1850. National Portrait Gallery, Smithsonian Institution.

conditions of workers in the North as well as in Britain. They were care-
ful observers of the European revolutions of 1848, which they perceived as
the triumph of liberty over authoritarianism.[43] "I deeply sympathise in this
grand movement resulting from the declaration of France to become a republic," Douglass declared in April 1848, applauding in particular the decision of the provisional government to speedily abolish slavery in the colonies. The "glorious consistency" of the French, he noted, "puts our own
country to the blush."[44]

Chautard's personal story encapsulates the ideological connections between the European "spirit of 1848" and U.S. radical abolitionism. Abolitionists in the United States, the historian Manisha Sinha writes, "viewed
the revolutions of 1848 . . . as kindred movements." They identified "their
own battle against slavery with European revolutionary struggles."[45] Pro-
slavery apologists were not entirely wrong when they claimed that "Abolitionists and Socialists [are] identical." "They are notoriously the same
people," the Virginian white supremacist George Fitzhugh thundered,
"employing the same arguments and bent on the same schemes."[46] Pro-
slavery interests rightly feared the "stimulating effect" 1848 could have
on U.S. abolitionism.[47] When they arrived in the United States in September 1857, Chautard, Paon, and Bivors were welcomed by the abolitionists. On November 8, Garrison wrote to the Transcendentalist activ-
ist Theodore Parker—the author of an 1848 speech on "The Abolition of
Slavery in the French Republic"—about the French socialists:

> Permit me to introduce to you [three] French refugees, who have had
> a marvellous escape from Cayenne, (the victims of the despotism of
> the French usurper, Louis Napoleon,) one of whom has with him an
> account of their escape . . . which cannot be read without the deepest
> commiseration for their unhappy fate. Is it in your power to suggest to
> them a mode to find friends or employment for the time being, until
> they can have time to adjust themselves to our usages? They will tell
> you their story, and I know that you will listen to it not only with re-
> spect, but interest.[48]

A few months later, in the letter quoted at the beginning of this introduction, Garrison reiterated his sympathy for the refugees, who were "homeless, penniless, friendless, strangers in a strange land, among a people of
strange speech." Their unequivocal condemnation of slavery in *Escapes*

from Cayenne caught his attention: Paon and Chautard did not fight only
for the cause of liberty in Europe but for that of "all mankind," and they
"argue for the rights of the black man as they do for their own."[49] It is
unclear whether the three French refugees ever met Garrison in person.
What is certain is that Garrison considered himself to be their protector
and helped to circulate their narrative. That *Escapes from Cayenne* boasts
on its title page the motto "Our country is the world; our countrymen are
all mankind"—the same slogan that adorned the masthead of *The Liberator* from 1831 to 1865—suggests that Garrison (or some other abolitionist
familiar with Garrisonian rhetoric) was directly involved in the production of the pamphlet.

Paon, Bivors, and Chautard were not the first French republicans who
sought refuge in the United States. Though Great Britain and the Channel Islands were the preferred destinations for French political exiles, a
number of dissidents ended up—with varying degrees of willingness—in
North America.[50] Eugène Quesne, Dominique Gourieux, Claude Cham-
bonnière, and Gustave Dime were all arrested after the 1851 coup and
transported to Guiana. Like Chautard, they were escapees from Cayenne
who found their way to the United States. Others, such as François Par-
digon, Henri Delescluze (brother of Charles), Claude Pelletier, Désiré
Debuchy, François Latour, and Victor Baron, were exiled first in Europe,
then in America. Fewer in number than their German-speaking counterparts, these French republicans mostly settled in New York, where
they formed a small community with its own political associations and
French-language newspapers such as *Le Républicain* and *Le Messager
franco-américain*.[51] French immigrants of diverse political tendencies
lived in New York, from conservatives who read the pro-Empire *Courrier des États-Unis* to the anarcho-communist Joseph Déjacque, founder
in 1858 of *Le Libertaire*. Some French-speaking immigrants, such as the
anarchist geographer Élisée Reclus, settled in New Orleans, an important
place on the map of the revolutionary Atlantic; in St. Louis, Missouri,
where the republican Louis Cortambert launched the *Revue de l'Ouest*
in 1854; and in Texas, which saw the establishment of several Fourierist
utopian communities under the leadership of Étienne Cabet and Victor
Considerant.

Chautard, for his part, settled in Boston, where French immigrants
were a very small group. He reentered the professional milieu of the

clothing trade, working for a retailer of "boots, gaiters and shoes" whom he supplied with articles made in Paris. In 1860, he returned to Paris on business, which must have provided him with the opportunity to see his wife and friends after over a decade of separation.[52] Chautard later abandoned the boot business for the glove trade and joined with several partners, including the appropriately named Goodsell and one Rickard— perhaps an exiled relative with an Anglicized name, since Chautard's mother's name was Ricard.[53] It is more difficult to follow the paths of Paon and Bivors. The former died in New York at an uncertain date, as another French exile reveals in his account. A "brave and humble soldier of democracy," Paon drowned "while attempting a rescue," making one final demonstration of his fearless and generous nature.[54] Bivors, who suffered from an affliction of the lungs when he arrived in the United States, likely did not survive long thereafter.

Political Violence and the Transatlantic Fight for Universal Freedom

The French exiles in the United States soon familiarized themselves with their new environment. Some, like Reclus in Louisiana, discovered firsthand the grim reality of slavery, which they deplored in their private writings but could not criticize in public; it was dangerous—not to say illegal—to do so in the South. In New York, republicans of all colors expressed antislavery views in the pages of French-language newspapers. Quesne, the editor of *Le Républicain*, found slavery to be "the great open wound of American civilization." He wrote, "It is a fault and a crime; it is an anomaly."[55] *Le Messager franco-américain* did not mince its words either when it came to the institution: "In whatever form it takes and whomever its victims, we detest slavery as a social vice, equally fatal to master and slave, incompatible with progress and the true doctrines of democracy and republicanism."[56]

These papers advocated not only for abolition but also for racial equality. "One cannot . . . be a friend of liberty without caring for equality," *Le Républicain* stated. Quesne rejected ideas of racial hierarchy and looked critically upon the segregation that prevailed in northern cities. He observed that "the line of demarcation is drawn everywhere, in theaters, churches, hospitals, cemeteries, and even prisons," where African Americans were "isolated . . . like lepers."[57] Writing from Missouri, Cortambert denounced the lynching of Black men.[58] The goals of antislavery and antiracism were by no means systematically intertwined in the antebellum United States, but the French socialists, like the abolitionists, saw them as two sides of the same coin. Admittedly, not all were attracted to Garrisonian abolitionism, which they felt was too imbued with religious sentiment; they would never have called slavery "a sin against God," a phrase commonly found in abolitionist newspapers. Quesne and Cortambert gravitated more naturally toward antislavery politicians such as Charles Sumner, Salmon P. Chase, and William H. Seward. Still, even those who felt at odds with the style and strategies of Garrisonian abolitionism shared its radical ethos—and recognized Garrison's talent.[59]

Chautard's close proximity with Garrisonian abolition set him apart. Indeed, by spring 1858, Chautard was sufficiently aware of who Garrison was and what he stood for to send a letter for publication in *The Liberator*. In an article published in the *Boston Journal*, some conservatives had expressed concern at the growing influence of "foreign Republicans" on the local political scene, whom they demonized as "levellers" bent on subverting the social order. Such attacks were common in the intensely xenophobic climate of the 1850s, which emerged as a backlash to recent waves of immigration made up of Irish fleeing the Great Famine and "forty-eighters" in exile. The article accused the French socialists of being "infidels in religion" and "inveterate enemies of Christianity."[60] It also complained about the poverty of the European migrants.

Chautard methodically countered such reactionary rhetoric in his response. If the French workers were so poor, he wrote, it was because "the social institutions of [France] are wrong; it is because they grant the greatest part of the produce to idle men, and nothing to the laborer." Socialists did not want to subvert the social order, rather the social order as it existed in France subverted "right, justice and equity." "We are called 'levellers,'" he went on, "but we are proud of this title. Yes, we are 'levellers,' and we are so because we sincerely think that, in modern societies, the social mountains are too high, and the social abysses are too deep." The conservative elite of Boston presented itself as the champion of what it called a "well-regulated liberty," but what did that mean in a country where "a perfectly dishonest association of three hundred thousand ruffians, liars and thieves" enslaved four million human beings?[61] Using purposefully religious rhetoric, Chautard affirmed the unity of mankind and launched into a diatribe against slavery:

> We believe that all men come from Adam and Eve; then we believe that all mankind,—white, red, yellow and black,—are *brothers*, and, as such, are born equally free. From which it results that it is an outrageous crime, a shameful, inexcusable robbery, to deprive anyone of his liberty, of the possession of himself. We believe that a man, made a slave, against the laws of nature, justice and humanity, has a right to reconquer by force his stolen property, his freedom. . . . [A] slave has a right to kill the master, who, by force, keeps him in bondage.[62]

By asserting the right of the enslaved to revolt against their enslavers, Chautard showed himself to be in step with the thinking of U.S. abolitionists who, after having long advocated the abolition of slavery by peaceful means, ceased to recoil from calls to violence. As Kellie Carter Jackson and Jesse Olsavsky have shown, Black activists, especially those involved in vigilance committees—antislavery organizations devoted to helping runaways along the Underground Railroad—played a leading role in this ideological and strategic shift.[63] The African American abolitionist James Rawson Johnson seemed prophetic when he affirmed, in an 1854 letter to Frederick Douglass, that the "needful work" of abolition would "come amid scenes of terrible and bloody revolution."[64]

Chautard's opinions on the use of violence should also be read through the lens of contemporary European politics. On January 14, 1858, the Italian revolutionary and patriot Felice Orsini, aided by three accomplices, attempted to assassinate Louis-Napoleon (or Napoleon III) while the emperor was on his way to the opera. The three bombs thrown at the royal coach wounded many and killed several, but the emperor and his wife were unharmed. This was not the first time (nor the last) that an Italian tried to kill the man who had ordered the invasion and destruction of the Roman Republic in 1849 and restored papal rule to central Italy. Three years earlier, Giovanni Pianori had shot twice at Louis-Napoleon with a pistol but missed him, as Paon recalls in *Escapes from Cayenne*. Pianori and Orsini were both executed, and the attack of 1858 led to the penal transportation of more republicans, including Charles Delescluze. In the same way that Chautard defended the right of the enslaved to rebel in his *Liberator* letter, he justified Orsini's use of violence against a tyrannical ruler: "Orsini and his companions had a right to kill Louis-Napoleon

Bonaparte, who had sent an army to enslave their native country."[65] The legitimation of political violence was here a common transatlantic thread linking Europe and the United States.

On April 29, 1858, the political refugees of Boston met at Turner Hall for a ceremony in honor of the martyred Italian. Republicans of all nationalities attended, including the Italian Francesco Piccaroli, the German Adolph Douai—and the Frenchman Léon Chautard. Each addressed the audience in his own language. A letter from Garrison was read and warmly applauded by the assembly. While reaffirming his belief in "the inviolability of human life," Garrison, a notable pacifist, declared that Orsini was "no assassin in spirit or purpose, but a brave man, true to his convictions of duty, his hatred of oppression, and his desire for the reign of freedom throughout Europe."[66] Like Chautard before him, he established a link between struggles against political oppression in Europe and the fight against U.S. slavery:

> Your meeting will receive no sanction from the American press, people, or government. How can America sympathize with any struggle for freedom in the old world? . . . With four millions of slaves in her ruthless grasp, she has not only lost all reverence for human rights, but she ridicules and rejects her own Declaration of Independence; and hence, her instincts and feelings are with every tyrant in Europe, and against its down-trodden masses; and such will be her state and attitude until she breaks every fetter, and liberates every slave, on her own soil: then shall she lead the nations of the earth to universal freedom.[67]

As the historian Mischa Honeck has noted, the radicalization of U.S. politics in the 1850s—notably the radicalization of abolitionists—often occurred with reference to European events, from the revolutions of 1848 to Orsini's assassination attempt ten years later. U.S. abolitionists did not just observe the uprisings in Europe: they learned from them and drew on them as a source of inspiration for their own struggles.[68]

This process worked both ways. In October 1859, the radical abolitionist John Brown launched his famous raid on the federal arsenal at Harpers Ferry, Virginia. Brown was well versed in revolutionary resistance to tyranny and slavery. At least one abolitionist, Thomas Wentworth Higginson, later stated that Brown wanted to "get together bands and families of fugitive slaves" and "establish them permanently" in the Alleghenies, "like the Maroons of Jamaica and Surinam," pointing to multiple interconnections between North America, South America, and Europe.[69] Brown had traveled to Europe in 1849, and among his associates were men sharing experience in the 1848 revolutions.[70] The raid failed, and Brown was executed on December 2—a highly symbolic date for the defenders of liberty in France, marking as it did the anniversary of Louis-Napoleon's coup. Many French political and literary figures took up Brown's cause, including Victor Hugo in the *London News*, the novelist and historian Marie d'Agoult (also known as Daniel Stern) in the regional French press, and the future Communard Pierre Vésinier in his 1864 *The Martyr to Black Freedom; or, John Brown, the Christ of Blacks*.[71] French-speaking exiles in the United States commented extensively on the event. Joseph Déjacque published a series of impassioned articles on the "martyred insurrectionist" in *Le Libertaire*.[72] It is likely that Chautard read avidly about Brown's raid and his subsequent execution.

The Harpers Ferry assault marked the final stage in the long march to civil war. The election of the moderately antislavery Abraham Lincoln as president in November 1860 set southern secession in motion. South Carolina was the first state to secede from the Union the following month. By April 1861, the country was at war against itself. A number of European political refugees, including some French exiles, fought for the Union, despite the neutrality that Napoleon III theoretically imposed on French citizens. Théodore Tassilier, a companion of Chautard in Algeria, Guiana, and the United States, enlisted in the 39th New York Infantry Regiment, popularly known as the Garibaldi Guard. He "breathed his last in America, during the War of Secession, in which he took part in the ranks of antislavery," wrote a fellow refugee.[73] Did Chautard take up arms during the Civil War? He intended to, at the very least. A brief article published April 22, 1861, in the *Boston Herald* stated that Chautard had set up a company of seventy-five French volunteers, and that he hoped to recruit thirty-five more. Much had changed since the attacks published against French socialists in 1858. "There are comparatively few Frenchmen in this city," the journalist wrote, "and their prompt action in defence of the flag of their adopted country speaks loudly in their praise."[74] It is unknown if Chautard and his volunteer company were actually involved in any fighting. It is clear, however, that Chautard saw enlistment in the Union army as another facet of a struggle for liberty and universal justice that began on the other side of the Atlantic. In 1848, he had participated in the revolution that gave birth to the Second French Republic. A decade and a half later, he participated in a war that was nothing less than revolutionary and gave birth to what historians have recently called the "Second American Republic."[75]

Returning to Gallargues

"Adieu, France, my native country, adieu for ever!" Chautard exclaimed in September 1852 as he left for Cayenne. Twenty years later, aged fifty-nine, Chautard permanently returned to the country that he never expected to see again. Like many of his more eminent counterparts, including Victor Hugo, Edgar Quinet, Alexandre Ledru-Rollin, Louis Blanc, and the abolitionist Victor Schœlcher, Chautard seems to have chosen to remain in exile even after the general amnesty of 1859 would have allowed his return to France. This decision gave his exile a distinctly political character, since to remain in a foreign land was to repudiate the legitimacy of the French Empire, even in its later liberal form. "One cannot amnesty truth or justice," Edgar Quinet declared. "I recognize no one's right to banish me or to recall me at their pleasure to my own country."[76] Chautard returned after the collapse of the Second Empire and the proclamation of the Third Republic—albeit too late to have participated in the Paris Commune.[77] After decades of struggle and separation, he doubtless aspired to a quiet life among friends and family. In the 1880s he lived in the city of Nîmes, in southern France, with his wife, Clémentine. The couple, it seems, never had a child.[78]

Yet Chautard never forgot his past trials and tribulations. In 1881 he even applied for a state pension as a former victim of Louis-Napoleon. The law of national reparation of July 30, 1881, allowed individuals to receive pensions if they could prove that they or their deceased parents or spouses had been punished by deportation, exile, imprisonment, or police surveillance for participation in the insurrection against the coup in 1851.[79] Over twenty-five thousand men and women applied. As someone who had been transported because of his participation in the June Days of 1848, Chautard did not technically qualify, and he hesitated to fill out an application, allowing the deadline set by the law to expire. On October 17, 1882, he finally sent a letter to the Minister of the Interior, which reads like a brief history of political repression in nineteenth-century France:

Monsieur le Ministre,

I have the honor of requesting to be included among the victims of December 2, 1851, and to share in the compensation that the government grants to those who have suffered for their attachment to the republican cause.

I was arrested in the street on July 11, 1848, and transported without trial.—My arrest was justified by the decree of June 27, 1848, which only mentioned *individuals currently detained* and therefore was not applicable to me.

I was *imprisoned* in the forts of Paris, on the ships of Brest, at Belle-Île-en-Mer, in Bône, Algiers, Oran and, finally, I was in Algiers at the time of the *coup d'état*. I was then sent to *Cayenne* where I arrived on November 1, 1852; I remained there up until July 13, 1857; I managed to escape at this time and sought refuge in the United States of America where I remained until 1872.

I sincerely hope, Monsieur le Ministre, that this simple review of the facts will suffice to include me in the distribution of pensions allocated by the government.[80]

As the French historian Louis Hincker argues, "The figure of the revolutionary and more still that of the 'insurgent' were no longer relevant" in the French political climate of the early 1880s.[81] Chautard therefore did not elaborate on his participation in the June uprising but rather insisted that he was transported "without trial" and by virtue of a decree that did not apply to him. There was, however, no political repentance or expression of guilt: he stood by his past positions. It appears that his request was denied.

Chautard's life ended where it had begun, in the village of Gallargues, where he returned in his old age and died on January 13, 1890.[82] Clémentine died two years later, on March 12, 1892, at a hospice in Nîmes.[83] Chautard had been to three continents and spent a third of his life as a transported prisoner and then as an exile. He left as a record of his transatlantic travels and revolutionary life a short pamphlet titled *Escapes from Cayenne*.

Nîmes le 17 Octobre 1882.

Monsieur le Ministre,

J'ai l'honneur de solliciter de votre bienveillance d'être compris dans les victimes du 2 Décembre 1851 et de participer à l'indemnité que le gouvernement accorde à ceux qui ont souffert pour leur attachement à la cause Républicaine.

J'ai été arrêté sur la voie publique le 11 Juillet 1848 et j'ai été transporté sans jugement. — On a motivé mon arrestation sur le décret du 27 Juin 1848 qui ne mentionnait que les insurgés détenus à cette époque et qui, par conséquent, ne m'était pas applicable.

J'ai été séquestré dans les forts de Paris, sur les pontons de Brest, à Belle-île en Mer, à Bône, Alger, Oran et, finalement j'étais à Alger lorsque eut lieu le coup d'état. On me dirigea alors sur Cayenne où j'arrivai le 1er Novembre 1852; j'y restai jusqu'au 13 Juillet 1857; je parvins à m'en évader à cette époque et me réfugiai aux États-Unis d'Amérique où je suis resté jusques en 1872.

J'ose espérer, Monsieur le Ministre, que cet simple aperçu des faits suffira pour me faire comprendre dans la répartition des indemnités allouées par le gouvernement.

Agréez l'assurance de ma respectueuse considération.

Léon Chautard

Vu pour légalisation
DE LA SIGNATURE DE Mr Léon Chautard Rue Neuve 2.
NIMES LE 17 octobre
1882
LE MAIRE DE NIMES

à Monsieur le Ministre de l'Intérieur
Paris.

Letter from Léon Chautard to the French Minister
of the Interior, October 17, 1882. Archives nationales.

Bearing Witness

Throughout his years as a prisoner, Chautard felt the urge to bear witness—to show the world what republicans had to endure in defense of their political convictions. In Algeria, he was able to publish an early account of his captivity in a local newspaper, *L'Atlas*, which led to his being placed in solitary confinement and then sent to the military prison in Bône. He also participated in editing an "Almanac of the Transportees" in 1851, a further sign of his interest in the written word.[84] Chautard then managed to pen another account of his life as a transportee while staying on St. Joseph Island, titled "The Dry Guillotine." First used by Tronçon du Coudray, a lawyer deported to Guiana in 1795, this phrase later gave its title to the best-selling memoirs of another—more famous—French escapee from Cayenne who found refuge in the United States, René Belbenoit (*Dry Guillotine: Fifteen Years among the Living Dead*, 1938).[85] Chautard sent copies of this second account to Belgium, England, and the United States, three nodes of the exiled republican diaspora. "I don't know exactly what became of them, but suppose they were published, having many reasons to believe so," he writes in *Escapes from Cayenne*.

It was perhaps an excerpt from "The Dry Guillotine" that appeared in August 1856 in *L'Homme*, a newspaper published in London by Hugo's friend Charles Ribeyrolles. Under the title "The Martyrs of Cayenne," the paper printed several excerpts from a manuscript sent by Chautard.[86] Two weeks later, the London *Times* published a letter to Louis Blanc signed by a large group of transportees that included Bivors: "At the very moment when so much is spoken in France of clemency and generosity, while so many families are lulling themselves with the hope of clasping to their hearts the dear ones whose absence they have so long lamented, the political victims are treated in French Guiana in a manner worthy of the darkest ages of barbarity."[87] The publication of *Escapes from Cayenne* should thus be understood as part of a continued effort on the part of Chautard, Bivors, and Paon to put into words the experience of imprisonment and exile and the hardships that it entailed.

A number of the French prisoners who were arrested after the 1851 coup gave similar accounts of their transportation to Algeria and Guiana. Some were published in book or pamphlet form, such as Delescluze's *From Paris to Cayenne*, Attibert's *Four Years in Cayenne* (1859), and Henri Chabanne's *Escape from Devil's Island* (1862). One of the most

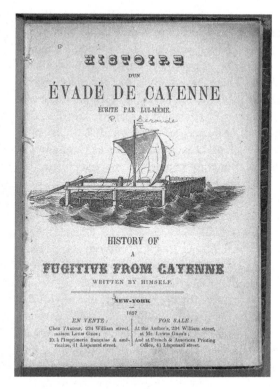

Title page of Pierre Séroude's *History of a Fugitive from Cayenne*. Widener Library, Harvard University.

visually intriguing memoirs may be Pierre Séroude's *History of a Fugitive from Cayenne* (1857), published in New York in a bilingual edition with the title appearing on the pamphlet's cover in both English and French.[88] The French- and English-language press offered another venue for such testimonies. U.S. newspapers in the 1850s often reported on what one New York journal called the "pitiful condition of French exiles" in Cayenne, and occasionally reprinted the letters they sent or translations of the lectures they gave after arriving in the United States.[89] An 1856 letter by Théodore Tassilier appeared in the *New-York Daily Tribune*.[90] "In the letter of M. Tassillier [*sic*]," wrote the *Tribune*'s European correspondent Karl Marx, "the reader will perceive the genuine story of the French citizens transported to Cayenne."[91] Other accounts, such as Dunaud's, were never published but survived in manuscript form.

Whatever form they took, these texts reveal how important it was for the prisoners to tell their stories. Penning one's transportation narrative was both a political necessity and a method of self-affirmation. When done in detention, it could serve as a way to pass the time or communicate one's fears or anger. Although these accounts are documentary in nature, they are also literary in the sense that they convey a particular subjectivity, style, and worldview. There are echoes in *Escapes from Cayenne* of such literary traditions as the picaresque novel (with its many embedded narratives) and Gothic literature (the most barbaric tortures are secretly administered in the Red Castle perched at the top of Royal Island). The building of the rafts by Paon and Bivors seems plucked straight out of Homer's *Odyssey*. Some accounts, of course, are more sophisticated than others: *Escapes from Cayenne* has none of the references to Tacitus, Byron, and Hegel with which Delescluze peppered his own memoirs. Yet its unadorned simplicity is precisely what makes it a powerful and moving record.

Published in the United States, *Escapes from Cayenne* can also be read as part of a local autobiographical tradition of personal narratives written by outsiders and people in marginalized groups. As Mechal Sobel writes, "In the eighteenth and nineteenth centuries, thousands of individuals, most of them of the middling sort or poor, including many at the margins, were enjoined or volunteered to write narratives of their lives."[92] Whether they were mechanics, murderers, beggars, prisoners of war, captives, impressed seamen, refugees, or enslaved men and women, the authors of these narratives all lived lives scarred by poverty, isolation, and violence. For some these conditions were permanent, for others they were concentrated in a single dramatic event or experience such as a kidnapping, a prison sentence, or an escape. Their lives were out of the ordinary, colorful, and often tragic.

With the exception of slave narratives, most such memoirs have been forgotten, though the formulaic structure of their titles resonates with modern readers: *The Narrative of Robert Adams, an American Sailor, Who Was Wrecked on the Western Coast of Africa, in the Year 1810* (1817); *A Narrative of Some of the Adventures, Dangers and Sufferings of a Revolutionary Soldier* (1830); *Narrative of the Life of Frederick Douglass, an American Slave, Written by Himself* (1845); and so on.[93] Many of the narratives were first-person accounts by people far removed from the world of the written word, let alone that of print culture, which is why they frequently include the words "written by himself/herself" on the title page.

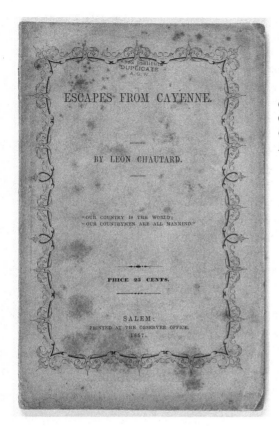

Cover of Léon Chautard's *Escapes from Cayenne*. American Antiquarian Society.

While this phrase is often seen as a defining feature of slave narratives, it was also found in the personal narratives of a variety of outsider authors, including exiles such as Pierre Séroude. The personal nature of these texts was underpinned by the way they were printed and distributed, with most self-published and self-marketed.

Escapes from Cayenne borrows from the tropes of this literature. Like other outsider authors, most of whom were native English-speakers but only amateur writers, Chautard apologizes for his limited command of the language in the introduction: his story will, of necessity, be told "in a plain style." Another challenge for such authors was to convince a potentially skeptical audience of the veracity of their tales. The back cover of Chautard's pamphlet lists fifteen citizens of Salem, who, by appending their names to his narrative, vouched for its authenticity. "The story of his trials and hardships . . . is deeply interesting," they claimed, "and told with unusual animation and spirit." Chautard and his companions, they also emphasized, had arrived in the United States "in utter destitution." Such narratives were indeed often penned by people in need, and authors (or their advocates) routinely appealed to the generosity of would-be readers. Purchasing a copy was presented as a charitable act. Wherever *Escapes from Cayenne* was sold, it was "for the benefit of these unfortunate refugees," as *The Liberator* made clear.[94] Thus *Escapes from Cayenne* was equally the product of U.S. and European literary traditions and textual practices.

Its circulation remained limited. Chautard wrote it rapidly in the days following his arrival in the United States, and it was first serialized in the *Salem Register* between September and November 1857. It then appeared in pamphlet form, likely with the financial help of one of the fifteen citizens of Salem mentioned above. A copy cost twenty-five cents. Garrison was the narrative's most active promoter. He advertised it in *The Liberator*, reprinting some of its most vigorously antislavery passages, and sent batches of twenty-five copies to several abolitionist friends and colleagues.[95] His wife Helen Benson Garrison also helped behind the scenes. As her children later reminisced, "On one occasion she went from store to store the whole length of Washington Street, selling the pamphlet narrative of a French political refugee who had escaped from Cayenne, until she had disposed of four hundred copies and thus made a hundred dollars for him."[96] Finally, *Escapes from Cayenne* was sold at the office of the Massachusetts Anti-Slavery Society, rubbing covers with autobiographical narratives of formerly enslaved men and women. Unlike authors of slave narratives such as Frederick Douglass, however, Chautard apparently did not do much for the dissemination of his own pamphlet, and the work soon sank into oblivion. More than a century and a half later, it is available again to U.S. readers.

NOTES

I would like to thank the following people for their help at various stages of preparing this edition of *Escapes from Cayenne*: Bernard Atger, Bryan Banks, Tristan Bellardie, Fabrice Bensimon, Charles Dupêchez, Véronique Fau-Vincenti, Marie Fleury, Alexandre Frondizi, Françoise Grenand, Pierre Grenand, Thomas C.

Jones, Elsa Juston, Nicolas Lawriw, Jean Moomou, and Gilles Poizat. Thank you also to Marie-Pierre Lajot and Chloé Pathé at Anamosa for publishing the original French edition, and to Jon Davies, John Gehner, and Nathaniel Holly at the University of Georgia Press for their work on the U.S. edition. This book is dedicated to my mother, Jacqueline Nacache.

1. Sylvie Aprile, *Le Siècle des exilés: Bannis et proscrits de 1789 à la Commune* (Paris: CNRS Éditions, 2010).

2. Mark Traugott, *Armies of the Poor: Determinants of Working-Class Participation in the Parisian Insurrection of June 1848* (Princeton, N.J.: Princeton University Press, 1985).

3. Charles Delescluze, *De Paris à Cayenne* (Paris: A. Le Chevalier, 1869).

4. Michaël Roy, *Fugitive Texts: Slave Narratives in Antebellum Print Culture*, trans. Susan Pickford (Madison: University of Wisconsin Press, 2022).

5. Letter from William Lloyd Garrison to an unknown correspondent, February 6, 1858, in *The Letters of William Lloyd Garrison*, vol. 4, *From Disunionism to the Brink of War, 1850–1860*, ed. Louis Ruchames (Cambridge, Mass.: Belknap Press of Harvard University Press, 1975), 510.

6. Quentin Deluermoz, Emmanuel Fureix, and Clément Thibaud, eds., *Les Mondes de 1848: Au-delà du Printemps des peuples* (Ceyzérieu: Champ Vallon, 2023); on the early American transnational turn, see, for instance, Seth Rockman, "Jacksonian America," in *American History Now*, ed. Eric Foner and Lisa McGirr (Philadelphia: Temple University Press, 2011), 61–65.

7. Archives départementales du Gard (Nîmes), 5 E 3006, 5 E 3005.

8. Victor Hugo, *Napoleon the Little* (London: Vizetelly, 1852).

9. "The French and German Volunteers," *Boston Herald*, April 22, 1861.

10. Service historique de la Défense (Vincennes), GR 34 Yc.

11. Alexandre Frondizi, "Paris au-delà de Paris: Urbanisation et révolution dans l'outre-octroi populaire, 1789–1860" (PhD diss., Institut d'Études Politiques de Paris, 2018), 17.

12. *Annuaire général du commerce, de l'industrie, de la magistrature et de l'administration* (Paris: Firmin Didot, 1847), 5.

13. Service historique de la Défense (Vincennes), 6 J 128.

14. Jonathan Beecher, *Victor Considerant and the Rise of French Romantic Socialism* (Berkeley: University of California Press, 2001), 2.

15. Samuel Hayat, *Quand la République était révolutionnaire: Citoyenneté et représentation en 1848* (Paris: Seuil, 2014).

16. Louis Ménard, *Prologue d'une révolution: Février-juin 1848*, ed. Filippo Benfante and Maurizio Gribaudi (Paris: La Fabrique, 2007), 125.

17. Letter from Léon Chautard to Joseph Sobrier, May 8, 1848, Archives nationales (Pierrefitte-sur-Seine), W 574.

18. Alphonse Lucas, *Les Clubs et les Clubistes* (Paris: E. Dentu, 1851), 233.

19. Letter from the Paris prefect of police to the Minister of the Navy and the

Colonies, February 16, 1853, Archives nationales d'outre-mer (Aix-en-Provence), COL H 569. On the National Workshops, see Jonathan Sperber, *The European Revolutions, 1848–1851*, 2nd ed. (Cambridge: Cambridge University Press, 2005), 153.

20. Ménard, *Prologue d'une révolution*, 202.

21. Service historique de la Défense (Vincennes), 6 J 128.

22. Letter from the Paris prefect of police to the Minister of the Navy and the Colonies, February 16, 1853, Archives nationales d'outre-mer (Aix-en-Provence), COL H 569.

23. See Charles Tilly and Lynn Lees, "Le peuple de Juin 1848," *Annales* 29, no. 5 (1974): 1069–70.

24. Letter from Clémentine Chautard to Louis-Napoleon Bonaparte, January 12, 1849, Service historique de la Défense (Vincennes), 6 J 128.

25. Véronique Fau-Vincenti, ed., *Des barricades à l'île du Diable: Journal de Jean-Baptiste Dunaud, révolutionnaire de 1848* (Ivry-sur-Seine: Éditions de l'Atelier, 2019), 103.

26. Quoted in Louis-José Barbançon, "Les transportés de 1848 (statistiques, analyse, commentaires)," *Criminocorpus*, January 1, 2008, https://journals.open edition.org/criminocorpus/148, loc. 11 and 12 of 42.

27. "Cours et tribunaux," *La Presse*, March 17, 19, 20, and 21, 1850.

28. See Allyson Jaye Delnore, "Empire by Example? Deportees in France and Algeria and the Re-Making of a Modern Empire, 1846–1854," *French Politics, Culture & Society* 33, no. 1 (2015): 38–39.

29. Fau-Vincenti, *Des barricades à l'île du Diable*, 145.

30. Delescluze, *De Paris à Cayenne*, 168.

31. Letter from Jacques-Eugène Leiris to Adolphe Labey, September 5, 1850, Bibliothèque Littéraire Jacques-Doucet (Paris), Ms 45138.

32. Archives nationales d'outre-mer (Aix-en-Provence), COL H 569.

33. Pierre Séroude, *History of a Fugitive from Cayenne, Written by Himself* (New York: French & American Printing Office, 1857), 14.

34. See Lawrence C. Jennings, *French Anti-Slavery: The Movement for the Abolition of Slavery in France, 1802–1848* (Cambridge: Cambridge University Press, 2000); Olivier Grenouilleau, *La Révolution abolitionniste* (Paris: Gallimard, 2017). On the state of French abolition studies, see also Nicolas Martin-Breteau's interview with Manisha Sinha, "L'abolition de l'esclavage, matrice des mouvements sociaux aux États-Unis," *Critique internationale* 80 (2018): 122.

35. "Pétition des ouvriers de Paris en faveur de l'abolition de l'esclavage," in *D'une abolition, l'autre: Anthologie raisonnée de textes consacrés à la seconde abolition de l'esclavage dans les colonies françaises*, ed. Myriam Cottias (Marseille: Agone, 1998), 127.

36. Aimé Césaire, *Victor Schœlcher et l'abolition de l'esclavage* (Lectoure: Le Capucin, 2004), 25.

37. Quoted in Arthur Lehning, "Une lettre de Joseph Déjacque," *Bulletin of the International Institute of Social History* 6, no. 1 (1951): 27.

38. François Attibert, *Quatre Ans à Cayenne* (Brussels: Veuve Verteneuil, 1859), 14; Fau-Vincenti, *Des barricades à l'île du Diable*, 82.

39. On Maroons in the Americas, see, for instance, Richard Price, ed., *Maroon Societies: Rebel Slave Communities in the Americas*, 3rd ed. (Baltimore: Johns Hopkins University Press, 1996); Alvin O. Thompson, *Flight to Freedom: African Runaways and Maroons in the Americas* (Kingston, Jamaica: University of the West Indies Press, 2006).

40. Attibert, *Quatre Ans à Cayenne*, 80.

41. Attibert, 100.

42. See, for instance, Walter Johnson, *River of Dark Dreams: Slavery and Empire in the Cotton Kingdom* (Cambridge, Mass.: Belknap Press of Harvard University Press, 2013); Edward E. Baptist, *The Half Has Never Been Told: Slavery and the Making of American Capitalism* (New York: Basic Books, 2014); Sven Beckert, *Empire of Cotton: A Global History* (New York: Alfred A. Knopf, 2014).

43. Manisha Sinha, *The Slave's Cause: A History of Abolition* (New Haven, Conn.: Yale University Press, 2016), 266–98, 339–80; W. Caleb McDaniel, *The Problem of Democracy in the Age of Slavery: Garrisonian Abolitionists and Transatlantic Reform* (Baton Rouge: Louisiana State University Press, 2013).

44. "French Sympathy Meeting," *The North Star*, May 12, 1848. See Benjamin Fagan, "*The North Star* and the Atlantic 1848," *African American Review* 47, no. 1 (2014): 51–67; Timothy Mason Roberts, *Distant Revolutions: 1848 and the Challenge to American Exceptionalism* (Charlottesville: University of Virginia Press, 2009), 84–87.

45. Sinha, *Slave's Cause*, 364.

46. Quoted in Sinha, 365. See also Roberts, *Distant Revolutions*, 113.

47. Jesse Olsavsky, *The Most Absolute Abolition: Runaways, Vigilance Committees, and the Rise of Revolutionary Abolitionism, 1835–1861* (Baton Rouge: Louisiana State University Press, 2022), 175.

48. Letter from William Lloyd Garrison to Theodore Parker, November 8, 1857, in Ruchames, *Letters of William Lloyd Garrison*, 499. For Parker's speech, see Theodore Parker, *The Slave Power*, ed. James K. Hosmer (Boston: American Unitarian Association, n.d.), 165–75.

49. Letter from William Lloyd Garrison to an unknown correspondent, February 6, 1858, in Ruchames, *Letters of William Lloyd Garrison*, 510.

50. On French exile to Great Britain, see Thomas C. Jones, "French Republican Exiles in Britain, 1848–1870" (PhD diss., University of Cambridge, 2010).

51. See Michel Cordillot, *Utopistes et exilés du Nouveau Monde: Des Français aux États-Unis de 1848 à la Commune* (Paris: Vendémiaire, 2013), 135–99; Marieke Polfliet, "Émigration et politisation: Les Français de New York et La Nouvelle-Orléans dans la première moitié du XIXe siècle (1803–1860)" (PhD diss., Université Nice Sophia Antipolis, 2013), 471–647.

52. *Boston Daily Advertiser*, October 24, 1860; *Salem Register*, May 31, 1860; *New-York Daily Tribune*, September 13, 1860.

53. *Boston Daily Advertiser*, November 6, 1866; *Daily Eastern Argus*, October 15, 1869; *The Massachusetts Register, 1869* (Boston: Sampson, Davenport, 1869), 496.

54. Jacques-Eugène Leiris, *Jadis* (Paris: Fourbis, 1990), 97.

55. "L'abolition de l'esclavage," *Le Républicain*, December 24, 1853.

56. Quoted in Charles Clerc, "Les républicains de langue française aux États-Unis, 1848–1871" (PhD diss., Université Paris 13, 2001), 490–91.

57. "L'abolitionnisme et l'égalité," *Le Républicain*, June 30, 1854.

58. "La loi de Lynch," *Le Républicain*, August 19, 1853. On Cortambert, see Anne Juneau Craver, "Louis Cortambert and *l'Esprit français* in St. Louis in 1854," in *French St. Louis: Landscape, Contexts, and Legacy*, ed. Jay Gitlin, Robert Michael Morrissey, and Peter J. Kastor (Lincoln: University of Nebraska Press, 2021), 243–70.

59. Clerc, "Les républicains de langue française aux États-Unis," 465–99.

60. "Conspirators' Bill in the United States," *The Liberator*, April 16, 1858.

61. "Conspirators' Bill in the United States."

62. "Conspirators' Bill in the United States."

63. Kellie Carter Jackson, *Force and Freedom: Black Abolitionists and the Politics of Violence* (Philadelphia: University of Pennsylvania Press, 2019); Olsavsky, *Most Absolute Abolition*.

64. Letter from James Rawson Johnson to Frederick Douglass, July 4, 1854, in *The Frederick Douglass Papers*, ser. 3, *Correspondence*, vol. 2, *1853–1865*, ed. John R. McKivigan (New Haven, Conn.: Yale University Press, 2018), 82.

65. "Conspirators' Bill in the United States."

66. "Orsini and Pierri Meeting," *The Liberator*, May 7, 1858.

67. "Orsini and Pierri Meeting."

68. Mischa Honeck, "'Freemen of All Nations, Bestir Yourselves': Felice Orsini's Transnational Afterlife and the Radicalization of America," *Journal of the Early Republic* 30, no. 4 (2010): 587–615.

69. Quoted in David S. Reynolds, *John Brown, Abolitionist: The Man Who Killed Slavery, Sparked the Civil War, and Seeded Civil Rights* (New York: Vintage Books, 2005), 107. Higginson also penned essays on Maroon resistance in Jamaica and Suriname, stressing Maroons' "creative strategies, military tactics, and their extraordinary ability to combat some of the most powerful empires of human history." Olsavsky, *Most Absolute Abolition*, 178.

70. Roberts, *Distant Revolutions*, 187.

71. On Hugo and Vésinier, see John Stauffer and Zoe Trodd, eds., *The Tribunal: Responses to John Brown and the Harpers Ferry Raid* (Cambridge, Mass.: Belknap Press of Harvard University Press, 2012), 367–72, 402. D'Agoult discusses Brown in an issue of *L'Avenir de Nice* dated December 17, 1859. Élisée Reclus, mentioned above, published a profile of John Brown in *La Coopération*, July 14, 1867.

72. "Prologue d'une Révolution: Les suppliciés," *Le Libertaire*, December 24, 1859.

73. Leiris, *Jadis*, 95. On foreign enlistment in the Civil War, see Don H. Doyle, *The Cause of All Nations: An International History of the American Civil War* (New York: Basic Books, 2015), 158–81.

74. "The French and German Volunteers," *Boston Herald*, April 22, 1861.

75. Gregory P. Downs, *The Second American Revolution: The Civil War–Era Struggle over Cuba and the Rebirth of the American Republic* (Chapel Hill: University of North Carolina Press, 2019); Manisha Sinha, *The Rise and Fall of the Second American Republic: A Long History of Reconstruction*, forthcoming.

76. Quoted in Sylvie Aprile, "Exil et exilés de gauche au XIXe siècle," in *Histoire des gauches en France*, vol. 1, *L'héritage du XIXe siècle*, ed. Jean-Jacques Becker and Gilles Candar (Paris: La Découverte, 2004), 194.

77. On the Paris Commune as observed from the United States, see J. Michelle Coghlan, *Sensational Internationalism: The Paris Commune and the Remapping of American Memory in the Long Nineteenth Century* (Edinburgh: Edinburgh University Press, 2016).

78. Chautard and his wife are listed in the censuses for 1881 and 1886. Archives municipales de Nîmes, 1F3, 1F6.

79. Stacey Renee Davis, "Citizenship, the Limits of French Identity, and Pensions for the 1851 Insurgents," *Proceedings of the Western Society for French History* 34 (2006): 178.

80. Letter from Léon Chautard to the French Minister of the Interior, October 17, 1882, Archives nationales (Pierrefitte-sur-Seine), F 15 4169.

81. Louis Hincker, *Citoyens-combattants à Paris, 1848–1851* (Villeneuve-d'Ascq: Presses universitaires du Septentrion, 2008), 34.

82. Archives municipales de Gallargues-le-Montueux.

83. Archives municipales de Nîmes, 3E 100.

84. Fau-Vincenti, *Des barricades à l'île du Diable*, 171–73. On republican almanacs, see Ronald Gosselin, *Les Almanachs républicains: Traditions révolutionnaires et culture politique des masses populaires de Paris, 1840–1851* (Paris: L'Harmattan, 1993).

85. Aprile, *Siècle des exilés*, 301; René Belbenoit, *Dry Guillotine: Fifty Years among the Living Dead* (New York: E. P. Dutton, 1938).

86. "Les martyrs de Cayenne," *L'Homme*, August 9, 1856.

87. "The French Political Prisoners at Cayenne," *The Times* (London), August 25, 1856.

88. Delescluze, *De Paris à Cayenne*; Attibert, *Quatre Ans à Cayenne*; Henri Chabanne, *Évasion de l'île du Diable* (Paris: Agricol Perdiguier, 1862); Séroude, *History of a Fugitive from Cayenne*.

89. "Pitiful Condition of French Exiles," *Brother Jonathan*, September 27, 1856.

90. "Letter from a Political Prisoner in French Guiana," *New-York Daily Tribune*, April 14, 1856. For a letter by a fugitive from Cayenne in the French-language press, see, for instance, "Les évadés de la Guyane," *Courrier des États-Unis*, January 7, 1853.

91. "Bonapartean Victims and Tools," *New-York Daily Tribune*, April 14, 1856.

92. Mechal Sobel, "The Revolution in Selves: Black and White Inner Aliens," in *Through a Glass Darkly: Reflections on Personal Identity in Early America*, ed. Ronald Hoffman, Mechal Sobel, and Fredrika J. Teute (Chapel Hill: University of North Carolina Press, 1997), 167. See also Ann Fabian, *The Unvarnished Truth: Personal Narratives in Nineteenth-Century America* (Berkeley: University of California Press, 2000); Karen A. Weyler, *Empowering Words: Outsiders and Authorship in Early America* (Athens: University of Georgia Press, 2013).

93. *The Narrative of Robert Adams, an American Sailor, Who Was Wrecked on the Western Coast of Africa, in the Year 1810* (Boston: Wells & Lilly, 1817); *A Narrative of Some of the Adventures, Dangers and Sufferings of a Revolutionary Soldier* (Hallowell, Maine: Glazier, Masters, 1830); *Narrative of the Life of Frederick Douglass, an American Slave* (Boston: Anti-Slavery Office, 1845).

94. "The French Exiles," *The Liberator*, December 18, 1857.

95. "Liberty for All Mankind," *The Liberator*, December 25, 1857.

96. Wendell Phillips Garrison and Francis Jackson Garrison, *William Lloyd Garrison, 1805–1879: The Story of His Life Told by His Children* (New York: The Century Company, 1889), 4:331.

A NOTE ON THE TEXT

Escapes from Cayenne was originally serialized in the *Salem Register* from September 28 to November 12, 1857. It was then printed as a pamphlet at the office of the *Salem Observer*, and this is the text used for the present edition. Editorial alterations have been kept to a minimum. Obvious typos (e.g., "Septembr," "unheaalthy") have been silently corrected. In a few instances, punctuation has been revised to facilitate reading. No attempt, however, has been made to improve or otherwise correct Chautard's occasionally faulty—though, on the whole, remarkably good—English. This edition retains the capitalization, spelling, and syntax found in the original.

Escapes from Cayenne

Preface

From the *Salem Register* of September 28, 1857

Within the past few years several of the French political refugees, victims of their Republican opinions, have found their way to this city from Cayenne, whither, after several changes of the place of their exile, they were finally banished. Those of them whom we have seen have been very intelligent and interesting men, and although evidently suffering severely from the weight of their sorrows and misfortunes, have borne up under them with wonderful firmness, evincing an earnest disposition to secure an honest living by their own industry, and an honorable sensitiveness at the idea of being dependent upon the kindly charities of sympathizing strangers for the means of support. Three of them are at present in Salem, having arrived within the past two weeks; and one, Mr. LEON CHAUTARD, a gentleman of intelligence and ability,—who hopes to procure employment in teaching the French language, until he can learn some tidings and receive remittances from France,—has sent to us a communication narrating the particulars of the escape of himself and his companions. Mr. Chautard escaped from Cayenne and his two friends from Devil's Island. The first narrative, he says, is singular; the second is wonderful, adding: "I send you the relation of these escapes. I know very well that they are badly written; but do not forget, Messrs. Editors, that I am a Frenchman, and have much difficulty to express my thoughts in the English tongue."

We do not think any apology is necessary, and give his narrative very nearly as he has written it, with only a few trifling alterations of the idiom.

Introduction

I wished to be able to describe, with a pen of fire, the atrocious crimes of the crowned Sycophant called Louis Napoleon Buonaparte.[1] Unhappily I am not well acquainted with the English tongue, and can only tell, in a plain style, the summary of the sufferings of some of Napoleon's victims. I respectfully beg the indulgence of my readers, and I commence:

In the month of February, 1848, Louis Philippe, King of the French, was driven from his throne and fled toward England, the refuge of all sinners.[2] The Republic was proclaimed with enthusiasm by the oppressed, and accepted with resignation by the oppressors; the throne of the Bourbons was publicly and solemnly burnt at the same place where stood, sixty years before, the State Prison called *La Bastille*.

Four months after this, day for day, the cannon was roaring again in the streets of Paris; the Republicans, disguised in Anarchists, were desperately fighting, for the sake of their freedom, against the Royalists of all colors, disguised in conservative Republicans; the regular army, tied by passive obedience, and the National Guard, deceived by the pompous speeches of the sublime poet and blind politician Lamartine, were both in the camp of the Royalists.

1 Chautard almost systematically uses the Corsican–Italian form of the name Bonaparte ("Buonaparte") as a way to undermine Louis-Napoleon's legitimacy as a French ruler.

2 Louis-Philippe reigned from 1830 to 1848. He lived in exile in England until his death in 1850.

After five days of a most furious and heroic struggle, the Republicans were vanquished. But the victory was dearly bought by the Royalists; eight generals were killed and six wounded; twelve hundred officers of all degrees, and twenty thousand soldiers or national guards, passed from life to death. All persons known for their devotion to Republican institutions were then imprisoned. I had the honor to be of the number, with twenty-five thousand more.

On the 11th day of July, 1848, I was arrested and brought before a commissary of police. The magistrate asked me, in exchange for my liberty, to give him my word of honor that I had not participated in the battle of June. I refused, saying, "I have not to prove my innocence, but you have to prove my culpability; I can be neither my own accuser nor my own apologist." I was sent to *La Conciergerie*. On the 21st of the same month I was removed to *Fort de Noisy*. On the first of September I was taken to *Fort de l'Est*. Two days before, a lady had begged my liberation of General Cavaignac.[3]

"In less than forty-eight hours, Chautard shall be out of the *Fort de Noisy*," answered the Dictator.

On the 2nd of September I was removed to *Havre*, and thence to *Brest*, where I arrived on the 5th. I was put on the pontoon *Uranie*. On the 19th of February, 1849, I was sent to *Belle Isle*, on the outworks of the citadel. On the 30th of April I escaped with Deflotte, a navy officer, and Clairet. Captured the next day, we had a dark cell for a residence, and we went, in May next, to *Lorient* to be tried. We were condemned to one month imprisonment. I made appeal and was sent to *Vannes* to be tried again.[4] The first judgment was confirmed. I was tried a third time for having insulted a non-commissioned officer of gendarmes. I was condemned again to one month imprisonment, and returned to *Belle Isle* in the month of August. On the 11th of December 740 of my companions were liberated; 460 of us remained. The weather being very cold, we made a good fire in our stoves, with the beds of our companions who had gone away. Our guardians called that an incendiarism, brought armed soldiers into our camp, and ordered us to go to bed. We refused and marshaled ourselves for passive resistance. The soldiers and guardians ran back and went to bring reinforcements. The whole regiment arrived. Their Colonel, quite drunk,

---

3 Eugène Cavaignac was in charge of the repression of the June insurrection.
4 Le Havre is in Normandy. Brest, Lorient, and Vannes are in Brittany.

ordered them to load their guns and to fix the bayonets. Several of us were wounded. In the evening I wrote to Col. Pierre; I clearly proved him to be a drunkard, a coward, and a murderer. The next day soldiers came again, shot one of us, wounded some, and arrested eleven. I had the honor to be of the last.

In January, 1850, we were sent to *Lorient*, ten in number, to be tried, and removed soon after to *Vannes*, before the criminal court. I wrote to my friends in Paris to send us defenders. We had the most eloquent Michel (de Bourges,) who had defended Louis Napoleon Buonaparte after his attempt at *Boulogne*,[5] Cassal and Baudin; all three were Representatives. [The last was killed upon the barricades, in December, 1851.][6] We had, besides, a renowned barrister of *Lorient*, named Rattier. They were sent to us by Count D'Alton-Shee, an old peer of France, the sole one who dared to condemn to death Louis Napoleon Buonaparte, when tried before the Court of Peers.[7]

The trial began on the 16th of March and lasted five days. I addressed the jury, but was interrupted fourteen times by the Attorney General. Tassilier[8] had addressed the public, and his pathetic speech had much excited the auditors; many of them, including barristers, were weeping. Michel (de Bourges) made the most magnificent speech I ever heard in my life; he proved not only our innocence, but also the culpability of our accusers. His thundering voice so far intimidated our persecutors, that no one dared to answer him. Forty-three questions were put to the jury; all were unanimously negatived, and we were acquitted.

When we left the Court House a crowd of people saluted us with enthusiastic hurrahs, and we were brought to our prison under the arms of our friends and covered with flowers.

But Louis Napoleon Buonaparte, then President, had reckoned without his host. Thinking we should be found guilty, he had transported our companions and sent them to Africa under the pretext of our culpability.

5 Louis-Napoleon Bonaparte made two attempts to seize power—first in Strasbourg in 1836, then in Boulogne in 1840—before his successful coup in 1851.

6 Alphonse Baudin opposed the coup of December 2, 1851, and was killed on a barricade the following day.

7 Edmond d'Alton-Shée, later a convert to republicanism, voted for sentencing Bonaparte to death after the attempted coup in Boulogne.

8 Like Chautard, Théodore Tassilier was arrested soon after the June Days. He was later transported to Algeria and French Guiana. He escaped from Cayenne in 1857 and settled in New York.

Being solemnly proclaimed innocent, the President's duty was to repeal the unjust law of transportation; but he preferred to do a new injustice— he sent us to join our companions in French Africa.

In the middle of the night we were taken by a company of grenadiers, assisted by gendarmes, and removed to an adjoining town called *Auray*; but there our friends were waiting our arrival, and we were immediately sent to the fortress of *Port Louis*. When, soon after, we left this place, two thousand persons wished us farewell, in such terms that we could not help our tears, and the remembrance of that day excites me much now, after seven years of incredible sufferings.

We made the passage from *Port Louis* to *Toulon*,[9] six hundred miles distant, in a cellular wagon, our bodies covered with irons. From *Toulon* we went to *Algiers*, and thence to *Bone*,[10] where we met our companions at the *Casbah*, or Citadel.—There, envy poisoned our triumph over our calumniators. Envy is the plague among the oppressed, as selfishness is the plague among oppressors. Which is the worst, Envy or Selfishness? Those abler than I may tell, but I cannot.

I published, then, the history of our confinement; when the first number went out, they put me in a cell; upon the appearance of the second number they sent me to the military prison of *Bone*. Six weeks afterwards I returned to the *Casbah*.

I introduced newspapers into the citadel, and, for this reason I was put in a cell where physicians declared that a man could not live more than three months. I remained there four months and two days and I was alive. The Commander of the Citadel paid me a visit, and told me he would kill me if I continued to publish the treatment I endured.

"I take notice of it, Captain, but I prefer to be a victim rather than a tormentor." For these words I was tried on the 4th of June, 1851, before a Court Martial, for insults to my superior. I refused to recognize Soldiers as my Judges, being a Citizen and not a Soldier. I was condemned to five years of irons, (a *military* punishment,) and sent to *Algiers*, to the cellular *civil* prison. Paon, Bivors, and many others, had the same fate, for trifling reasons, and joined me.

We had three cents a day for our board, and these three cts were given to the keeper of the prison, who stole half of it; we were starving and

---

9   Toulon is a port city on the Mediterranean coast.
10 Bône is now known as Annaba.

slowly dying. I preferred to die immediately, and absolutely refused to eat whatever it might be. A physician came, felt my pulse, smiled and said: "By-and-by he will ask for food; hunger will be stronger than his will." "Doctor," said I, calmly, "you are wrong to believe it: there is a loaf of bread; it is near my hand, and consequently, near my mouth, but I will become a corpse before that bread shall be touched; they must change the diet of the prisoners or assassinate me."

On the fourth day of my fasting, the Editors of Algerian Newspapers and some of my political brethren were admitted into the prison; they begged me to take some food. I asked them if the diet was modified. They called the Governor of the prison, who said to me: "I have orders to give you what you like."

"And my friends?"

"All political prisoners will be treated as you are."

"And the whole of the prisoners?"

"We cannot change the diet for soldiers, sailors, prisoners for debt, &c."

"Then let me die."

"But if you die—"

"There will be a soldier less for my party and a crime more for yours." A few hours afterwards the diet was changed for the prisoners, without any exception, and I tried to eat something, but I could not. I underwent a severe sickness, but my good constitution saved me. We had but a little profit from that event, having been removed to *Fort Barbazoun* a short time afterwards.

During our residence at this fort the President of the Republic made his *coup d'etat*; he drove the Representatives before the bayonets of his soldiers, confined many Generals, and drowned all the public liberties in an ocean of blood. The Phantom of the Republic was standing up yet, but every one could count the number of days it had to live. We were sent to *Fort St. Gregoire* at *Oran*. We had, there, a little less than two cents a day for our living, and our washing was to be paid over that sum.

One day my companions were singing Romances, and I was reading on my bed. The keeper ordered my friends to be silent; they refused, as was their right,—the commander of the fort having given them permission to sing and to speak.—The keeper arrived with twelve soldiers, armed to the teeth, with fixed bayonets. I told them to go back, having nothing to do in our room; the keeper called me a rascal and a brigand; I struck him in the face. The sergeant of the soldiers tried to give me a blow with his bayonet, but I prevented it and struck the sergeant's nose; I then jumped backward to prevent five or six bayonets shining around my breast. The keeper drew a long dagger and raised it above his head. I immediately uncovered my breast and told him: "Strike if you dare," and I looked earnestly, deeply into his eyes. The rascal could not bear my fiery glance; he was willing to kill me, but his arm could not move. A soldier then took him by the neck and told him in a thundering voice: "I will strangle you if you don't instantly put your dagger in your pocket." The wretch obeyed and went out. This good soldier had two months of dark cell, and I was condemned again, by a court martial, to five years of irons for insults to my superiors. After two months of separation I was reunited to my companions. During my absence some more had arrived, and Tassilier was among them. We received orders to leave *Fort St. Gregoire.* We inquired where we were going to; they refused to tell us, but I knew it as well as themselves: our destination was Cayenne; Mr. Louis Napoleon Buonaparte had condemned us,—by his private authority,—to the *Dry Guillotine,* as Lamartine, clear sighted now, calls the transportation to French Guiana.

We left *Fort St. Gregoire* and were directed toward *Mers-el-Kebir,* the sea-port of Oran, five or six miles distant. Our friends held a subscription for us, and sent one of them to give us the amount of it. The commander of our staff took the money and put the bearer in jail. [Our friend staid two months in prison and the money was never recovered.] Indignant at this officer's conduct, we denounced it in angry terms, and the soldiers, exasperated by our just reproaches, menaced us with their guns and bayonets. From *Oran* to *Mers-el-Kebir,* we were many times near being massacred; and we had no arms, and our hands were tied with chains!

We embarked on board a steam man-of-war and went to Algiers for the third time. The commissary-general of police made a search in my luggage; his agents looked at my papers and in my trunk and found nothing wrong; they asked their chief if it was of any use to search my person. "No," said he, "I know the man, we will find nothing; leave us alone."— The agents obeyed.

"Mr. Chautard," said the commissary general, "if you had followed my advice you would not be in such a position as you are; you would be free; but there is time yet; beg the Prince Napoleon's pardon, ask for mercy, be devoted to the President, and you will be liberated. You have no fortune, but you can keep a lucrative office. Will you do what I say?"

"No, sir."

"You have no faith in the President's promise, but you are wrong; the Prince is good hearted; he remembers that Commodore Chautard brought his uncle, the great Napoleon, from *Elba Island* to France, and exposed greatly his life by doing so; he remembers that two of your uncles, your mother's brothers, two valuable officers, died bravely in the campaign of Russia; he remembers, too, that your—"

"I only remember, sir, that I never had offended Louis Napoleon Buonaparte when he put me in prison,—against the laws of my country,—and treated me as a mad dog. Therefore I cannot beg his pardon without shame and dishonor. I shall not do it."

"But the Prince is President of the Republic, and you are but a poor prisoner; if he has been wrong with you, he cannot confess it."

"He will do as he likes, let his destiny and mine be fulfilled!"

"Is this your last word?"

"Yes."

Orders were given to let my companions stay in Africa, but, by a special favor, I was destined to be sent to Cayenne. The next day I embarked for *Toulon*. It was in the month of July, 1852.

The 5th of September,—I never shall forget that date,—I left France, and I swore never to come back again to it; but I was much excited; my eyes were fixed upon the Mediterranean shore where I was born, and I exclaimed with a deep sorrow:

"Adieu, France, my native country, adieu for ever!

"Adieu, cherished companions of my youth, I shall see you no more!

"Adieu, my black eyed and black haired lady, whose love and devotion bore up my fainting courage, in many circumstances, and made my happiness for many years! those whom God had united are separated by men. But God is merciful and men are mortal! Perhaps we shall meet again; thy beautiful eyes, O my lady! will look into mine, thy pretty rosy lips will kiss mine!—No, no; all hopes are lost, the sacrifice is done; adieu, my beloved, adieu forever, but remember me!"

I am on board the *Fortune*,—what a mockery!—three hundred convicts are on board and satisfied that they are going to Cayenne;—what a pity!—We cross the straits of Gibraltar, the Tropical line, the Equatorial line at the mouths of the Amazon river, and we arrive at French Guiana on the last day of October, 1852.

On the 4th day of November I went to the Jail at Cayenne; but I had made a sacrifice above my strength and I fell sick; I entered the hospital. A black melancholy invaded me and during forty days I became more and more disheartened. At last, I succeeded in regaining my self-possession, I resolved to live, and overthrow my sorrows. I asked the Doctor to let me leave the hospital; he said I was not strong enough; I insisted and he finally let me go.—They brought me to the Jail.

The Doctor had knowledge of it and asked the Governor to allow me to reside in the town of Cayenne. The Governor refused at first; but, several gentlemen having supported the Doctor's request, I left the Jail and had the town for a prison. I entered the General Navy-stores to fix its books.

Louis Napoleon Buonaparte made himself Emperor of the French, and, on that occasion, his newspapers offered liberty to all political prisoners who would recognize his nomination.—We had a new Governor sent to Guiana. I wrote to him that I accepted the bargain of his master and recognized the accomplished event of his election, to make me free or to send me to the United States of America.

Instead of giving me what I asked for, the Governor sent me to a dark cell for forty days, on *Mother Island*.[11] I found there about two hundred political prisoners, of the category of December, 1851.

In July, 1853, we received one hundred companions from France and Africa; Paon, Bivors and Tassilier were among them, and I was in a dark cell. On the 21st of the same month, I was with Paon and another friend, on a desert place of Mother Island, making a boat for our escape. When we arrived in the camp, at sunset, we found everything overthrown.

During our absence, some gendarmes had brought on a bad quarrel with our companions, and, reinforced with the soldiers of the garrison, attempted to massacre them; but the prisoners, far from being intimidated, had pressed the soldiers so closely that they could not move and use their guns. The cells were filled with our companions, and there were sentries in every quarter of the camp. Mother Island was proclaimed to be in a state of siege.

11 Mother Island is an islet off the coast of Cayenne.

In August, twelve of our fellow prisoners were tried before a court martial. Paon was amongst them. Three—Tassilier was one—were condemned to five years of irons; two others to two years of imprisonment; and Paon was acquitted.

We were sent to St. Joseph Island and treated worse than convicts; we were covered with chains, while the thieves, and the murderers of the *Bagne* had none; we worked the whole day under a tropical sun, and were not allowed to light any fire nor to cook any thing. On Sundays we filed off before a second lieutenant of marines; the Roman Catholics were obliged to go to mass, and the Protestants to stand up before the chapel, the face turned to the sun.

We stayed at St. Joseph Island for nineteen months, and lost fifty of our companions—the fourth of us. They died from despair, want of food, ill treatment, and dysentery. I wrote there a manuscript, entitled: *The Dry Guillotine*, and succeeded in sending out three copies, one to the United States, one to England, and the third to Belgium. I don't know exactly what became of them, but suppose they were published, having many reasons to believe so. In that work I related all the particulars of our sufferings, and the bold robberies of our tormentors.

In the month of March, 1855, the Governor of French Guiana, Rear Admiral Bonard, came to St. Joseph Island and informed us that our *hard labor* was suppressed, and that we should be removed to Devil's Island, where we could do as we liked.

At the beginning of April, M. de la Richerie, Governor of Salute Islands, visited St. Joseph and ordered me to accompany him to Devil's Island.[12] When we were alone in his boat, he asked me to beg the Emperor's pardon.

"I will support your request, and the Governor will advocate it," said he; "you are quite sure to receive your liberation by return of mail."

"I can not do such a thing, sir."

"Why?"

"Because I am not the offender; I am the offended."

"Don't mention it; ask for pardon and they will give it to you."

"I never shall."

---

12 Chautard twice refers to *les îles du Salut* as "Salute Islands" instead of "Salvation Islands" (*salut* means both "salute" and "salvation"). The Salvation Islands are St. Joseph Island, Royal Island, and Devil's Island.

"Then you will stay in prison all your life."

"Never mind."

M. de la Richerie asked me if I would direct the erection of the nec-essary buildings, at Devil's Island, for the whole of my companions. I ac-cepted on condition that we should have neither soldiers, nor gendarmes, nor policemen with us.

"But you must have administrators."

"Nobody."

"But if there are quarrels among you?"

"We shall not quarrel."

M. de la Richerie accepted my condition, left me at Devil's Island, and on the next day many of my companions joined me. In five weeks we erected thirteen *Cazes* wide enough to lodge three hundred men, and we were but one hundred and fifty political prisoners in French Guiana.

When I left Cayenne, two years before, the Governor said to my friends that I should return there in a few months; but, every time they required him to fulfil his promise, he always found pretexts to decline it. He was changed, and his successor did the same.

A respectable merchant, though a Portuguese, begged of M. Durand, the Director of the Penitentiaries, to let him have me as his clerk; but he refused obstinately. He confessed I was honest and intelligent, but he added: "All the political prisoners may come to Cayenne, except the one you ask for."

For these reasons I thought it quite impossible to leave the islands, and was most astonished when M. Durand's son-in-law called for me and said:

"Will you go to Cayenne?"

"Yes, sir, I am willing."

"When will you go?"

"The sooner the better."

"Then write to any worthy person to become bondsmen for you, and you may go."

"I will do it, sir."

I did, and three days afterwards I was called to Royal Island and went to Cayenne. When I arrived there, Gov. Bonard told me this:

"Leave us quiet, and we will leave you quiet."

"I never brought you any quarrel, Governor."

"Be still—be still."

Louis Napoleon Buonaparte had an heir—monsters are sometimes fertile—and the *Moniteur* proclaimed an amnesty for the political prisoners on certain conditions.[13] I accepted them, and presented my acceptance to M. de la Richerie, the Director of the Penitentiaries.

"It is not very flattering," said he, "but I will send it as it is."

Governor Bonard left Cayenne, and we had M. Baudin instead of him. The latter was a coarse seaman, fond of liquors and with a passion for money; he was ruled by his wife, and she was ruled by her minions—so that French Guiana was in the hands of young, foolish men, who used to do everything wrong, when I took occasion to make my escape.

In the following pages I relate my own, and the escape of some of my companions. We are now in the United States, waiting for a better future, trying to forget the past, and thinking not too much about the present, which is dull and hard.

Leon Chautard.

---

13 The "imperial prince" was born on March 16, 1856. *Le Moniteur universel* was the official journal of the French government.

Escape from Cayenne

I have been in prison for Republican opinions for nine years, and in Cayenne for five. I was tired of being treated like a slave or a criminal, and was resolved to run away from that country where dying is the rule and to live the exception. But it was very difficult to execute my project, because I was much in suspicion and many eyes were open and fixed upon me. Notwithstanding the difficulties, I was unwilling to stay any more in the power of my cruel enemies, who are too cowardly to kill their antagonists, and too thorough haters to forbid any offence.

In the mean time an English bark entered the harbor of Cayenne, loaded with coal for the French government, and her charter party stipulated that she would deliver her cargo in Cayenne or Demerara, at the French Governor's will.[14] I knew she was to sail for English Guiana the following night; so I had no time to spare, and I spared none. By means I can not tell now, I was on board the English bark at nine o'clock in the evening, and an hour after my arrival we sailed. We had high water, a fair breeze, and were running pretty well. I was saved; I was the happiest of men; I most heartfully thanked God and went to bed. I was sleeping very soundly when I was awakened by Captain Foskey.

"Friend," said he, "we are on a bank of mud; we are stopped and can't go away."

The captain, mates and crew tried, by every means, to move the ship,

14 A former Dutch colony, Demerara was part of British Guiana in the mid-nineteenth century.

but all was in vain; they lost an anchor and a rope. Capt. Foskey was very sorry for that accident, and so was I.

"Captain," said I, "I must die or be saved; please to make a hole in the deepest part of your ship, put me in, give me bread and water, nail a board over my head, and let me become what will please God."

All those things were done by Capt. Foskey himself and his brave and intelligent first mate, Mr. Tutton, a good natured young man.

The entrance of my voluntary prison was very dark and very narrow; it looked something like a wild beast's den. In entering it I scratched my clothes and a little of my skin; but I didn't take notice of it. My liberty depended on my willingness, as you will see by-and-by. Next day, at high tide, the captain paid me a visit.

"We have plenty of water," said he; "the ship is floating, but we have no wind at all; the sails are flat against the masts; we don't move."

"Blow, wind, blow!" cried I; "blow very hard and deliver me." But it appears that heaven is too far from earth; God heard me not, and we had no wind.

In the evening of the same day we had a very strong breeze. I heard it blowing from the bottom of my den, and I thought to be saved; but, alas! there was not sufficient water for our heavy ship, and she moved no more than a stone. Capt. Foskey was desperate; I was not, but I was dull like a mourning day.

It was almost impossible for me to stay any longer in my hole. I had room enough, but I had no air, and there was such a heat there that I was as wet as a duck when he is coming from the water. I was, besides, almost suffocated. Good Mr. Foskey engaged me to go into his cabin.

"Nobody will come to-night," said he; "come with me; you will sleep on the sofa, and to-morrow at daylight, we will see what we have to do."

I accepted his offer and followed him. I slept perfectly well in his cabin, and was breakfasting with him and Mr. Tutton, at about 8 o'clock, when a strong voice cried on deck:

"A white boat coming from shore, full of police men."

I immediately left bread and butter, cold meat and hot coffee, and ran to my den. In the way I heard a sailor saying: "Another boat coming from shore—she is full of gendarmes." I ran quicker and arrived at the hole. Capt. Foskey went himself with mate Tutton, and they nailed the board over my head. Five minutes afterwards, policemen, gendarmes, soldiers, Garde-Chiourmes, sailors, and spies of all descriptions jumped on the deck of our ship.[15] As no one of those vile and mercenary men could speak English, an old man was with them as interpreter. They begged leave of Capt. Foskey to visit his ship, and asked him if he had not seen a political prisoner recently escaped from Cayenne.

"I know nothing about that," answered the captain; "I arrived here in the morning and left the place in the afternoon. I am acquainted with nobody in Cayenne; and as to prisoners, I would not, for one thousand pounds sterling, help any one to run away. You can do on my ship what you like; this is not my business;" and he turned his back to the Mouchards.[16]

They instantly proceeded to visit the ship, went into the cabin and looked in every where, but found nobody. They went on deck, jumped over the masts, looked in the sails, and finally asked Mr. Tutton to let them see into the casks where was the salt meat. "Steward," said the young man, "bring me the keys; those men are in want of a piece of pork;" and he opened one of the casks, but there was only salt meat in it. Garde Chiourme asked Mr. Tutton to look in the other one. "Very well," said the mate; "I see what it is; you don't like pork and are fond of beef; it is very easy to satisfy your appetite." He then opened the beef barrel, and taking a large piece of salt beef, he put it on the fancy dress of a Garde-Chiourme. All the crew laughed, and the poor spy went away.

The infernal troop entered the Sailor's Cabin and looked into empty hogsheads, chests, etc. One of them told his comrade: "Call Chautard by his name, perhaps he will answer you." "He will do nothing of that kind," said another; "he is not so foolish as you may believe." "You are quite right, my good man," said I to myself; "I will do like the Capons when a cook calls them; they used to run away and they do well; I cannot run, but I will be still, and as mute as a fish." A *sergent de ville* found a pair of boots and shook them, in the hope, I believe, to find me inside; but I was not there. During that time, gendarmes, sailors, and soldiers invaded the coal; they sought me in every corner; I was entirely surrounded by those devils; four or five times they went so near me that I thought to be discovered and murdered by those assassins-like. I had a very good American revolver in my right hand, well loaded, with five shot, and I had a good will

15 *Chiourme* is prison slang for "convict." A *garde-chiourme* is a prison guard.
16 A *mouchard* is a spy.

to kill the first ones who would attempt to seize me. Happily for them, more happily for me, no one saw me and they went out.

They came three times, and every time, I thought to be found. I was not, and after a few hours of searching, all returned to Cayenne.

I went on the deck and threw my revolver into the sea. "I regret," said I, "to have had the intention to kill any one for my own sake. I will never do it again. If I am discovered I will be killed, that is sure, but I will die as I have lived, without reproach."

I stopped a full week in the same position. A Pilot went on board with four negroes and stayed three days; during these, I was obliged to be in my den, and the ship stopped on the bank of mud.

At last the Governor of Cayenne, requested many times by Captain Foskey to send a steamer to relieve his bark, sent a man-of-war. We left the corrupted Cayenne, its convicts and its martyrs, its Garde-Chiourmes, the mud and the yellow fever.

We rapidly passed Devil's Island, a small rocky islet, where about forty or fifty of my companions are dying slowly. The sight of their tomb moderated my selfish happiness, and my thoughts became as dull as before.

After two days of sailing, with a strong fair wind and close weather, the ship stopped once more in the night; we were on the mud again. "All hands on deck!" said a commanding voice, and, two minutes after this order was given, it was executed by all the men. This time we were not on the bank of mud which runs parallel with the shore, from Cayenne to Demerara; we were too far from land for that. The Chevalier (that is our ship's name) was in a patch of mud, and her position was not critical at all. Capt. Foskey, by a very skilful manœuvre, which consisted in turning around the patch, disengaged his ship, and we got away for the third and last time.

We enter the river of Demerara. I can distinctly see both banks; the shore is very low, and the water, in color and thickness, is like chocolate. On our left lies Georgetown, in the county of Demerara, and capital of the whole of British Guiana.

I land with Capt. Foskey; nobody, gendarmes, soldiers, or policemen, asked our passports, as they are accustomed to do in my country. I am well satisfied with this, for the good reason that I have none to exhibit. In France they surely would put me in prison; here, they take no notice of me. I prefer the English fashion. In France, Custom House officers would look in my pockets, in my hat, in my shoes, in my stockings, to see if I have or have not any newspapers, books, prohibited goods or infernal machine. They would ask me my christian name, my family name, and my nick name; they would take good care to see if I have not a double skin purposely made to hide a Ledru Rollin's pamphlet or something of that kind.[17] In Georgetown no one pays the least attention to me. English manners are positively better than French, I must confess.

Capt. Foskey introduces me among his friends and acquaintances. I am welcomed every where. Many captains of English ships ask me different questions about my confinement in France, in Africa, and, lately, in Cayenne. I answer the truth, no more than the truth, but the entire truth. They are indignant at my oppressors' conduct, and they pity the sufferings of French Republicans, who, in February, 1848, granted a sublime pardon to their enemies, and who, four months afterwards, in June, 1848, were so indignantly and shamefully treated by them. The very same men, when victorious, have been proclaimed unconquerable heroes by the whole press; when vanquished, they have been called thieves, murderers, incendiaries, by governmental and venal newspapers, Constitutionel, Assemblee Nationale, and many others.[18] Poor France! in what hands are you fallen!

English captains offered me to take my board and lodging in their ships, but I declined this kind offer; I had some money, and would not increase my obligations too much. They were quite willing to carry me to England without any expense, but I refused this too. I am very grateful to Capt. Foskey, mate Tutton, and the whole crew of the bark Chevalier, for what they have done for me; they have saved my liberty and my life; I never will forget it. I shall not forget, either, the honest captains, their countrymen.

I had two things to look for: the first one was to inquire if there was, in Georgetown harbor, any ship ready to sail for the United States of America, where I wished to go; the second was to inquire if any of my political brethren, escaped from Devil's Island, were in the country. I began with the first. I met an American captain who told me he was to start for Baltimore on the following day. He asked me sixty dollars for my passage. I answered it was rather dear.

17 Alexandre Ledru-Rollin was a radical politician and leader of the revolution of 1848 who was forced into exile.

18 *Le Constitutionnel* and *L'Assemblée nationale* were conservative newspapers.

"That's not dear at all, sir," exclaimed the captain; "and if I consent to take you for fifty, that will be very cheap indeed."

"That is cheap enough for you, captain, but that is too dear for my pocket; I can not give such a price."

"Well, sir, come with me; let us see the American Consul, and I hope we will make a bargain to our mutual satisfaction. Come."

I followed the captain. A fine looking gentleman is the Consul of the United States in Demerara; he received me very kindly and said he sympathized with my misfortunes, but could do nothing to assist me. "My Government refuses to pay the expenses incurred in helping French Republican refugees to go to the States. See M. Peraudeau, the French Consul," added he; "tell him to come with you, and we will try among the merchants to do something for you."

I had little desire to meet the French Consul, and I tried another way. When I was in Cayenne I had been acquainted with a merchant of Demerara; I had despatched one of his ships without charging him one cent for my trouble, and I hoped a good reception; but I was quite mistaken. The merchant received me more than coolly and left me alone in his store. At first I was astonished at his conduct, but I remembered he was a *Jew*, and I exclaimed, laughingly: "That man belongs to a people who, in olden times, killed God's son; he has a right, in modern times, to be ungrateful and clownish—that is a progress, and a good one; in future he will become as polished as a Russian or Turk."

I resolved to see M. Peraudeau. I entered a watch-maker's shop; an elderly lame man received me and said: "My son, the Consul, the representative of the French Emperor, has not arrived yet; wait a moment; he will soon be here." I waited half an hour. I was thinking, and my thoughts were painful. "What do you want?" said a fife-like piercing voice; "who are you?" I looked up and could not help laughing. I saw a thin, pale man, no bigger than a riding stick, with a face like a fox's muzzle; he had a trick which consisted in trying, when speaking, to bite both of his ears. His clothes were more ridiculous, if possible, than his person; he had a blue dress coat, twice too large for his body, with ornamented metal buttons. I thought he was an English footman, but he was M. Peraudeau.

I made known the desire of the American Consul. "I can do nothing for you," said M. Peraudeau; "you are not a Frenchman—you have lost your rights of French citizenship."

"If I had lost nothing else, I should be richer than I am, because there are no rights in France now, except the right of obedience; there are no laws except the law of force."

This was my answer, and I immediately left the shop. M. Peraudeau is the French Consul in an English colony; he speaks French like a Spaniard, and speaks English worse than a German. Poor France!!!

I was told that several Republican refugees were in Demerara, and employed at the place called the fort, at the end of the town. I went there and found my friends, two of whom had been my faithful companions for many years. Arrested at the same time, we had been separated in Algiers. We met again in the islets of French Guiana. Separated once more at Devil's Island, we were reunited a second time at Demerara, and this time we were all free.

I had the most cordial reception. They guided me to their home and we supped together. After supper we took a walk, Paon on one side, Bivors on the other, and I in the middle. We talked about our captivity, our friends, our hopes and our escape. I gave them an account of mine, in the same manner that I have done here, and, when ended, I asked them how they had managed theirs. "That history," said Paon, "is long and wonderful; our escape is a miracle; we are tired, so are you; let us go to bed; to-morrow I will stay all day with you. We will have plenty of time to speak about such things. You have no clothes, but you can make use of mine; my lodging is yours, my purse is yours; I am very poor, but I don't care for myself, I only care for you." Bivors told me the same and gave me some money. I had more in my pocket than he had in his, but I accepted, being unwilling to displease him. I was much affected by that sincere and friendly reception.

I went with Paon to his room. I entered first, without any accident, and my friend followed me. He was in the middle of the small wooden bridge which separated his door from the street, when a plank turned over his foot and he fell into the ditch. He arose alone and entered the room, telling me that he had a pain in his left arm. I looked at it and saw his shoulder was broken. I told him the truth. "This is a trifle," said he; "it is too late to call a surgeon; let me sleep; at daylight we will think about it."

We tried to sleep, but we could not, Paon suffering from pain and I being too much excited by the first smile of liberty, and pleased at meeting with my two companions.

We rose up, lighted a candle and talked about our mutual adventures.

Paon manifested to me his desire to know what I had done during the time I had been in the town of Cayenne.

"I will satisfy your curiosity, my good friend," said I, "and I will do it in a few words. You remember I left Devil's Island on the 10th of May 1855; I arrived in Cayenne the same day and was perfectly well received by a gentleman, who obliged me to exchange my uniform of convict for decent clothes. I made a package of the former and threw it into the sea in the hope that I never again should wear them. A discounting bank was to be established in Cayenne.—I entered it as clerk, opened its books and formed its capital against the Minister of Marine instructions. That minister was an able admiral, a perfect seaman, but he knew nothing about book-keeping and financial matters.

"In three months the bank was instituted. Then they took three clerks; one of them was an old officer who had a good pension and was Superintendent of Burials; he possessed, beside, four or five valuable buildings in Cayenne and three plantations in the country. Being in want of nothing, they gave to him the best wages. The second was an insane man; but he was a brother of the Director of sappers and miners. He is in the Insane Asylum now. The third clerk was the most lazy fellow I ever met in my life, but he was the Mayor's son. As to poor Chautard, they told him to procure another situation, being quite useless in the establishment. An old and rich man employed me as his secretary; he called himself a Philanthropist and a Socialist, but he lent his money at the rate of thirty-six per cent per annum. I could not agree with the old miser, being quite unable to comprehend his philanthropy. At that time they put me in jail for two months for having called '*Slave Dealer*' a man who was, in fact, a retailer of negroes. I entered a wholesale provision house as book-keeper, corresponding clerk, salesman and translator of English. I was pleased with my situation, but I was obliged to leave it by the Governor's orders."

"What had you done for that?" inquired Paon.

"I had done nothing. The most honorable merchants of Cayenne, (Mr. Fabens at their head,)[19] indignant at the Governor's conduct concerning the 'Gold Diggings,' had denounced his treacheries to his Government. The Governor could do nothing against these gentlemen and he avenged himself upon me."

19 The Fabens family were involved in the commercial trade between Salem, Massachusetts, and Cayenne.

"He told you," said Paon, "to leave your situation and get another?"

"He told me nothing at all. That should have been a gentleman's fashion, but French Governors are not obliged, now, to be gentlemen—he sent me two gendarmes who put me in jail."

"And you were in a cell quite alone?"

"I was amongst convicts, amongst anthropophagi, amongst men who, having escaped from penitentiaries, had killed and eaten three of their companions, in the woods."

"The necessity of living had obliged them to be so ferocious?"

"Not at all, my dear Paon. When these cannibals killed and ate their companions, they had plenty of provisions; they had rice, biscuit, pork and sweet potatoes."

"And you slept among such people; and you didn't fear to be killed and eaten?"

"I feared nothing. I am too old, too tough and too thin to be eaten; my flesh couldn't be made tender, boiled nor roasted."

"What did they do with these rascals?"

"They were executed; they mounted on the scaffold eight days after I had left their odious company."

"That is horrid," said Paon; "that is horrid and cowardly besides; but I am not astonished at the Governor's conduct; when he went to Devil's Island, he told us this: 'You shall work, and work very hard; you shall work, and work harder than convicts. And, if you refuse to work, I will kill you like mad dogs.'" Mr. Baudin is a very eloquent man.

"After you had left business, what did you do?" asked my friend.

"I entered the sappers and miners' office, as book-keeper. Many and many times I attempted to run away, but I never could succeed with American ships; every time that one of them was ready to sail, I was put in jail, on different pretexts, until she had left Cayenne."

"How many political prisoners remain there now?" continued Paon.

"There are about fifteen yet," said I; "all the others are gone to France, escaped or dead."

"What are the last events in France and in Cayenne?"

"In France there is nothing new; every one is calm, and that calm announces a very near tempest. Cayenne is very quiet; there is nothing new, except a heavy robbery lately discovered."

"Oh! ho!" said Paon, "robberies are common in Cayenne, that is nothing new."

"You are right, my dear friend, but the robbery I am speaking of is not a common robbery;—it was made by a high officer's hands;—the treasurer general filled his pockets and emptied the government's boxes."

"He was tried before the criminal court, I suppose?"

"No!"

"He will then go before a court martial?"

"Not at all! This man is quietly walking along the streets, more haughty than ever, his Cross of the Legion of Honor on his breast. When he is passing, soldiers, inferior officers and sentries render him the military honors."

"But that man gave back the money he had stolen?"

"He gave not one cent. The money is still in his pocket."

"But somebody paid it for him?"

"That's true. Merchants who supply the Government with provisions of all kinds, and contractors, (they were interested to save such a man, every one knows what for,) paid, amongst them, the six thousand dollars he had stolen."

"And the magistrates said nothing?"

"They told the magistrates to be blind and mute, that affair not being within their jurisdiction."

"But the Ministers, the Emperor, can't help giving orders to pursue the thief!"

"Under the reign of a Highwayman, such things as robberies are very lawful. Don't you recollect that Mr. Louis Napoleon Bonaparte, on the 2nd of December, 1851, sent the 32nd regiment of the line to the Bank of France, to obtain five millions of dollars? His followers do as he has done. In diplomacy they call that 'borrowing money,' but we call it, in our rough language, 'an armed burglary.' I have done with these turpitudes. Now, Paon, tell me of your wonderful escape."

"I am quite willing, but let me tell you, first, some preliminary particulars of my life as a political prisoner."

Paon's Narrative

"A short time after you had left Devil's Island, we built, some ten or twelve of us, a boat; she was made ready, supplied with provisions, sails, oars and masts. We attempted to launch her, but she broke her bottom on the breakers.

"We held, then, a general meeting, in which we requested the whole of our companions to build a schooner large enough to carry all of us. The motion was unanimously adopted.

"Love of liberty gave us strength and skillfulness. In a very short time we had built a large and beautiful schooner of 65 feet in length. We hoped to be saved; but, alas! our poor schooner had the same fate as the boat, and her remains would clearly show to our guardians, at daylight, what were our intentions. To prevent this, we used the night to demolish her, and brought the remains, piece by piece, to a secret grotto.

"We did not lose hopes of escape. We constructed two small boats, more solid than the first. They were nearly ready made when one of us, a coward, a spy, informed our guardians of our projects. The next day a party of soldiers, accompanied by policemen and sailors, came to our island. Soldiers stole the whole of our provisions; policemen searched in our chests and took what pleased them; and sailors seized our boats and brought them to Royal Island, where resides the Governor of the three small islands called Salute Islands, of which Devil's Island is one. We were unlucky, indeed, but we were not discouraged; and our betrayer being dead, soon afterwards, we saw in that event a Providential advice to continue our attempts of delivery.

"To build any more boats was quite impossible. We had neither boards nor planks, nails nor tools. We resolved to make rafts, and in that purpose we were looking for materials, when I was kindly invited to go to Royal Island in a dark cell for two months, and in the pillory for fifteen days."

"I thought, Paon, that the pillory had been abolished a long time ago?"

"You are right, Chautard; the late Governor of Guiana had suppressed thick iron rings on our legs, long chains, heavy cannon balls, the horrid pillory, and all these infamous, monstrous things; but I have been put, notwithstanding that, in the pillory; and I must describe to you what the pillory is."

Paon was interrupted by the arrival of Bivors, who said that a surgeon was waiting to look at his wound. My two friends went out, and I remained alone, much excited by Paon's account.

My friends were absent two hours. When they came back again into the room, they told me that the surgeon had advised Paon to enter the colonial hospital, because his wound would make him unable to work for six weeks. Paon was resolved to follow the surgeon's advice, not having money enough to pay the expenses of a treatment at home. Bivors and I were very sorry for it, but we could not help it, being nearly as poor as he. Paon could not go to the hospital before the afternoon; then he continued his recital as follows:

"At the top of Royal Island is a very spacious building called the Red Castle; the first and second floors of which are barracks for the soldiers of the garrison. The level ground is divided into two parts by a large passage; on each side of this passage are several small doors, with a square hole on the upper part and big bolts in the middle. Inside of each door there are a wooden camp-bed and a window of two feet high and two inches wide. The first door on the left, (when entering the passage,) introduces to the guard room; the other doors introduce into cells. [I am well acquainted with these apartments, having been lodged here for one year; I know the whole of the cells, having occupied all of them, one after the other.][20] In the middle of the passage are five or six machines, standing in a right line like soldiers; they are made with four strong wooden feet and a round piece of wood fixed in their middle; this piece is about six feet in height, three in circumference, and has iron rings behind it. These machines are called pillories.

20 Chautard's comments on Paon's narrative are bracketed.

"I was sent, as I have said, from Devil's Island to Red Castle. When I arrived inside the passage, my two leaders left me and took, in exchange for my person, a receipt in good order. The castle keeper ordered me to undress myself.—When I was in the same condition as Venus rising from the waves, the Cerberus opened a door, put me inside, locked it outside, and began to examine my clothes with a most particular attention. I asked the three-mouthed dog if he intended to make a bargain with me for the whole of my goods. 'I will accommodate you well, my good animal,' said I.

"'Silence!' said he, severely; 'don't joke with an imperial officer when he is exercising his honorable functions.'

"Cerberus pursued his examination. He carefully took tobacco, snuff, pipe, knife, scissors, thread, needles, paper, ink, pen, pencils, silver and copper money, pin, etc., and carried the whole into his kennel. At his return he threw me my clothes and said:

"'Don't speak, don't sing, don't whistle, don't make any noise, but you can do everything else.'

"I was at the door, looking through the hole into the passage, when I saw the tormentor of convicts coming hastily with big ropes in his hands. My cell was opened, and the castle keeper required me to go with him.

"'Where to?' said I.

"'On the pillory for a fortnight.'

"'I refuse, I positively refuse to go with you.'

"'You cannot refuse without giving reasons.'

"'I have many good reasons for my refusal, and the first is this: the pillory is abolished. I think it useless to tell you the others.'

"'I don't care; I have received orders to put you on the pillory, and you shall go, willingly or by force.'

"'I shall go by force, perhaps, but I never will go voluntarily.'

"'Help, soldiers, help!' exclaimed the keeper.

"Immediately five or six soldiers and the convicts tormentor invaded my cell; the guardians ordered me to follow them. I refused obedience and ran under the camp-bed. Then began a furious wrestling between me and my persecutors. They vainly attempted to carry me out; I had put my arms and legs around the feet of the camp-bed, and it was possible to break my limbs, but it was not to disengage them. The keeper and the tormentor took the soldier's guns, and with the butts they struck my hands and feet. My flesh was mangled, my blood was running, but I did not leave the feet of the camp-bed.—The soldiers, indignant at this sight, refused to let them continue any longer; they took their guns from the keeper's and the tormentor's hands and ordered them to be quiet. They called four more of their comrades, and all together, succeeded in carrying me out of the cell without injuring me. For my own part, I was quite unwilling to strike any of them; I only made a passive resistance. I was drawn to the pillory. They ordered me to stand up alongside the middle piece. I refused to obey. Then Jack-Catch[21] took me by the beard and the keeper passed a rope around my body; the sergeant passed the rope through the top ring, and, some of my persecutors pulling the rope, some others pulling my beard, they raised my head to the top of the mast. I was unable to resist any longer, having lost in the struggle all of my strength, half of my beard, and much of blood. The tormentor then joined my feet upon a foot of the pillory, and tied them hardly four or five times with a rope, and tied the rope itself to the lower iron ring. A second rope was passed around my body and vigorously tied by the tormentor, assisted by the keeper and the sergeant, both of whom put their feet on the mast and pulled the rope with both of their hands, while the former was tying it to the middle ring. I had a third rope crossing my breast. A fourth rope tied my neck most closely on the top of the mast, and was fastened at the top ring. I was strangled, I was suffocated, I could not take my breath, and my stomach was so furiously oppressed that I could not help doing—what I cannot say.

"I had to be in such a position for two hours, twice a day, for fifteen days! I could not bear such horrid sufferings, and I was there but a short time when I saw the walls turning over and I fainted. When the two hours were ended they untied me, but I was like a corpse, and they were obliged to bear me into my cell.

"One of the soldiers was born in Paris, my native place, and had been my neighbor; he pitied me. They sent him to prison for one month.

"And do you know what I had done to be thus condemned to the pillory? My crime was this: I had laughed most heartily when the Governor of Royal Island had sent soldiers and policemen to Devil's Island, on purpose to seize what they tho't to be a boat full of prisoners escaped from Cayenne. When the policemen arrived at Devil's Island, they saw very distinctly that the supposed boat was a large tree carried off by the current, and the supposed prisoners were the branches of that tree.

---

21 John Ketch, generally known as Jack Ketch, was an infamous hangman in seventeenth-century England. His name is used as a generic term for an executioner.

"One afternoon, while I was on the pillory, the guardian dared to endeavor to induce me (he had superior orders for that) to submit to the Emperor, his master.

"'If you consent,' said he, 'you will be liberated both from prison and pillory—you will be a free man.'

"So did the Devil to Jesus. 'Go to ——,' said I, roughly; 'go to ——, and your master too; I never was tried; I never have seen a judge; consequently, no one has a right to keep me in prison.'

"'Tormentor,' quietly replied the keeper, 'tie Paon a little tighter.'

"About forty of my yoke-fellows have been put on the pillory. Among them all, only one, (M. Tassilier, who was in Salem three weeks ago, and who is in New York now,) only one could bear that atrocious martyrology without fainting; on the contrary, he defied his persecutors the whole time he was there.

"Shame, shame forever to those who, in a civilized age, order such ignominious things! Shame to those who, being leaders of a civilized nation, are shameless enough to permit such barbarous treatment! Shame to Louis Napoleon Buonaparte, who, having been himself a political prisoner twice in his life, forgets the sins of his youth, and accepts the responsibility of such shameful tortures! You have a bad memory, M. Louis Napoleon Buonaparte, but mine is good. I remember that, in 1851, I wrote you these words:

"'In the beginning of the next year you will kill your mother, the French Republic, and you will be Emperor until the month of April, 1858.'

"You killed the Republic in December, 1851, and soon afterward you was proclaimed Emperor. You ought to be satisfied. You have been married and you have an heir—you ought to be delighted. But the year 1858 is near, very near us, and you will fall in the course of that year; not like Charles the Tenth, with dignity; nor like Louis Philippe, with the disdain of the people. You will fall poorly, like a vulgar wheedler, by the act of your soldiers, whom you have accustomed to have no faith, no honor, no honesty, to betray their oaths; they believe neither in God nor in Devil. You will gather the fruit of the seeds you have propagated in their hearts. Your soldiers, some morning, being tired of you and having nothing else to do, will put a rope around your neck, and the next tree will avenge your numerous victims."

Our conversation was interrupted by Bivors, who said it was time to go to the colonial hospital.

Paon handed me a manuscript, in which his escape was related. It was written in French; I have translated it into English—that is all. I give that relation exactly as I received it.

Leon Chautard.

August 25th, 1856.

I was put in prison without any judgment, in the month of June, 1848. Since that time I have been travelling through the world like the Wandering Jew, and, from prison to prison, from cell to cell, I am arrived at the granite patch called Devil's Island.

Every thing is dull around me. On my left is Royal Island, the residence of the criminal; on my right is St. Joseph Island, where I was so miserable for two years—where I had, for eighteen months, a large iron ring on my leg, with big chains twelve feet long, and ended by a cannon ball weighing twenty-five pounds—(I was working the whole day, *gratis pro deo*,[22] with these jewels, and I slept with them;)—where I had dry bread for my eating, stagnant water for my drinking, and eighteen inches of room for my lying down, (and I am under the equatorial line, too, remember!) Before me, just opposite, is Kourou, where twelve thousand of my countrymen died of famine, under the reign of Louis the Fifteenth, the corrupt monarch.[23]

For how long am I in this place? I don't exactly know, but I think it is for all my life. Nothing but my death can satisfy my cruel enemies; nothing but an escape can deliver me. Then I must escape or die. Death is a trifle for a man so miserable as I; I have seen death very near me many times without fear. Death would be the end of misfortunes. But dying on that rock, six thousand miles from my country, without a friend to close my eyelids! Dying banished, disdained, calumniated, and afterwards to be food for shark; dying as forty-two died, the other day, and were thrown into the water! What a strange fate is ours! When alive, they refuse us a stone for our pillow; when dead, they refuse us six feet of ground for our tomb. Dying without a tomb, where a friendly hand might, every Spring,

22 "Freely for the love of God." Used ironically to mean that the work is unpaid.

23 In the 1760s a colony was established in Kourou under French sponsorship. Most of the colonists died, and the remainder returned to Europe.

deposit a fresh flower, where a blue eye might spare a tear! No, no, that would be too horrid! No, no, I cannot die here—I am not willing to die—I shall not die.

I must escape, then. Yes, I must escape; but I am unlucky in my attempts; I tried many times in France, many times in the three provinces of Northern Africa, many times in the islets of Southern America, and I never was fortunate enough to succeed. What matters it? I must escape, and I shall escape.

September 1st, 1856.

We have resolved amongst us to make rafts for our escape. At first the enterprise seemed to be almost impossible, but it is become easier. They intend to favor our island with gendarmes once more; but our poor looking cottages are not handsome enough for those lords, and they require us to erect a palace for their dwelling. We affect to accept, and they will send us materials for that purpose; and among these materials will find something fit to make rafts with. Our enemies are blind or insane; they believe we have forgotten their cruelties and our sufferings. We will escape—we will escape!

September 6th, 1856.

They sent us two days ago, some long pieces of wood. We have now sufficient materials to construct two rafts, from twenty to twenty-five feet in length. The wood is very heavy and could not float, but we have a large quantity of maize quite ripe; with the stalks of these plants we have made bundles and tried them on the sea; a bundle of thirty sticks can bear a man. We will put on each raft a sufficient number of bundles to bear men, provisions, luggage and wood, and everything will be right.

Our materials are all ready, though remaining yet in their respective places; in a few hours, all hands working, we can make the rafts. We have no sails, but our shirts being sewn together will give us some; we have no ropes, but we can make some of the fibrous bark of the palm tree. We should be able to run away to-night if these preliminary things were done; but, as they are not, we will make our escape next Saturday.

September 13th, 1856.

To-day is the great day, the day of deliverance; to-morrow I shall be free or dead. If so, I will die like a man attempting to escape. I am much excited; my blood runs quickly through my veins; my head is burning, and my heart beats violently in my breast. I can not stay two minutes in the same place, and I cannot walk.

Time seems long to-day. Our guardians used to visit our island three times a week, Tuesdays, Thursdays and Saturdays; to-day is Saturday, and they are not yet come. Perhaps they are suspicious and will prevent our escape!

Two boats are starting from Royal Island, and there are many persons in each. They are coming in our direction, and they move very quick; they seem to be in haste to arrive. No doubt we are discovered—we are lost! I have nothing to do but to dash my head against a rock.

Policemen are landing; they are more numerous than they ever were; they look at everything; they search in every place. God of the oppressed, protect us!

Policemen are walking very slowly; they don't leave Devil's Island; what is the matter with them? do they intend to stay here all their life? God be thanked! they are gone away; their boats are far, very far; they go farther every minute—we are saved!

At the same time all hands are required to assist us; all hands are heartily working. Some carry the pieces of wood; others are making bundles of maize; a party is employed to demolish a cottage purposely erected with maize, between the bundles of which are concealed the few planks found in the island. Another party cuts down a tree, clears it of its branches and make a mast. Many are sewing shirts, and we have sails; many others are making oars. Every one is useful, according to his strength and skillfulness.

All right, brethren, all right, every thing is ready! Our two rafts are floating and provisioned; we have nothing to do but to ship and sail.

This moment is the most solemn of my life. Thirty-four of us are designated to embark, (our rafts can not bear more,) and fifty-five to stay at Devil's Island. The former are grave but determined; the last are dull but resigned. They embrace us, and many can not help a solitary tear. "If you escape, brethren," say they, "avenge our memories, assist our widows and our orphans, and we will die satisfied."

At half past seven P. M. we start from Devil's Island; twenty of us are on the largest raft, and there are fourteen on the smallest. I am the only seaman amongst both crews; the others are quite unacquainted with the sea, but several of them were boatmen on rivers. I will manage the sail of the large raft, and a boatman sits at the helm, which is a large oar. The weather was very calm the whole day, but it becomes rough, and we expect a tide-gate, so dangerous in this latitude, but it is too late to go back; we must escape or die. If we can gain ground enough to be in full sea at the strength of the race, we will be saved; otherwise we shall be capsized and all drowned. Then go on, boys, go on and make haste.

The small raft leaves the shore; she floats well and goes gently. We endeavor to do the same, but our oars are defective, our oarsmen unskillful, and our raft is heavy. We cannot stem the current and we drive upon Royal Island. The wind increases, the sea becomes higher, and the moon arises from the water. By and by we shall be perceived by our guardians and caught, or dashed against the rocks. Boldness, only boldness can save us. I raise our sail, but I miss the breeze; I quickly try again, and this time I am more fortunate; our sail swells, full of wind. We run uncommonly well, and in a short time we are alongside the small raft.

"How imprudent you are!" said a man of her crew; "by raising your sail our guardians can see us."

"I could not help it," I reply.

"Then we can raise our sail, too?"

"Do what you like, and let us do what we like."

The small raft raises her sail and we keep company together. It was time, full time to do so, the wind being strong and the sea very rough. Besides that, we have fourteen of our men very sick and quite unable to assist the six others.

September 14th, 1856, 6 o'clock A. M.

We are at the entrance of Sinamary gulf, stormy at all times and dangerous in rough weather. The small raft is not far from ours, and runs as well as we do. We examine most attentively both of them; they are in good condition. The land is out of sight, but we suppose ourselves to be thirty or thirty-five miles from shore. We have neither compass nor spy-glass. We continue our way, the big raft ahead, the small one behind.

Seven o'clock. We are inside the gulf, the sun is brilliant, the sky beautiful; the wind is high and the sea is roaring; we roll much, but we move quick.

"Help, brethren, help!" cry those on the small raft; "we are sinking!"

I immediately put down the sail and wait for our companions. When they are at a short distance I ask them what's the matter with them.

"We heard a cracking noise on our raft; she is too slender for her loading; please to take five or six of us on yours."

I look at the raft and see that she is in good order. "Brethren," I say, "your raft is good; she is perhaps better than ours, and you have nothing to fear. What you require, it is impossible to do; you are but fourteen on yours, and we twenty on ours; but follow us, and if we see you in any danger we will give you assistance." We raise up the sail and run again.

Eight o'clock. The weather is worse than ever, the wind blows furiously, the sea makes a dreadful noise, and the waves are as high as hills; we roll violently and fear to be thrown overboard. The small raft suddenly turns her head in the direction of the shore; we go straight as before. Our provisions are spoiled, our bread is quite wet, and our spring water is mixed with salt water. The waves bring our poor raft from their top to their bottom with an incredible velocity; when at their white summit we see the small raft running rapidly to shore; when in their dark abyss we see nothing but heaven and the two walls of roaring water. Our companions experience painfully the effects of sea-sickness; they can not move, and that is a lucky chance for the whole of us, because if they could, they doubtless would go all together to the same side of the raft, and they would oblige her to turn over.

Twelve o'clock. We are outside the gulf, the weather is a little better, and the sea is quieter; we cannot see the land, but we distinguish the small raft, which becomes smaller and smaller.

Four o'clock. No land, no raft in sight, nothing around us except the blue sky and the green sea.

September 15th, morning.

Since four o'clock, yesterday evening, until now, we have had nothing new; our raft is not too much damaged by the storm, she can keep the sea; but we are very tired, not having slept for two nights; we are hungry and have nothing to eat, but we don't take notice of it, having acquired the habit of hunger in our several prisons; we are thirsty and have no fresh water, but our feet and the lower part of our body are in the sea, and this circumstance diminishes our thirst. We see the land at about twenty miles on our left, and that sight brightens our hopes of liberty. The wind was fresh all night but for a couple of hours it has been sinking, and if that continues any longer we shall have a calm, the most grievous thing for men in our situation.

2 o'clock P. M. We have no wind, not the smallest breath; there are no waves, nor the least wrinkle on the sea—it is as plain as a looking-glass; the sun is exceedingly hot and burns our heads; the thirst is parching our throats, the hunger is imperious and devours our stomachs. We are in that state for a few hours only, but it seems to have been so for many years. We are quite silent—no one of us utters a word, no one dares to proffer a murmur, but we are looking one at the other, and our eyes are more eloquent than our lips could be. In order to complete our griefs, we perceive in the distance a thick cloud of smoke, which is formed, without doubt, by the chimney of a steamship. Our persecutors have dispatched a man of war in pursuit of us.—Elements and men combine their strength against us; we must combine ours against them.

"Oh! brethren, oh! put down the sail, take the oars and pull towards the shore; we must strive with might and main to escape our enemies."

5 o'clock P. M. One hour ago a small breeze began to blow, and we have a strong wind now. We are trying by all means in our power, to gain the open sea, because certain infallible signs announce to us a hurricane, and it is less dangerous, in those circumstances, to be far from than near the shore. The steam man of war, our pursuer, is far ahead and out of sight; we prefer that; as she goes a great deal quicker than we do, we don't fear her approach.

7 o'clock P. M. The hurricane is now in all its strength. We could not carry sail and have put it down; we could not steer and our helm is lying down; the darkness is thick, the noise is horrid, the water is hissing, the abysses are wide open, the waves pass over our heads, nature is overthrown, and our poor raft goes at God's pleasure. We cling to her with our hands, we raise our hearts to the mighty Creator of all things, and we let our destiny be fulfilled without useless despair, but with little hope of escaping.

Midnight. The hurricane is pacified, and the sea is not quite so furious. We look around us and see but water and sky; we don't know where we are, we don't know where we go to; we raise our sail, we take our helm, and we steer our shattered raft approximately to the west.

We are sailing for three or four hours when we perceive moving lights; we suppose them to be near land and go towards those lights; they become more and more distinct; they are very near, so near that we see human shadows on shore.

"Come this way, sirs, come this way," says a manly voice in good French, free from any foreign accent.

"Go away, go away and make haste," I whisper to our pilot; "go away quick; this is a French land, and gendarmes are on shore."

We immediately try to go back, but we can not do so; the wind is against us, and the current and the tide too.

"Come this way, sirs, come this way," repeats the voice.

"Down with the sail, boys, and up with the oars; row energetically," I say to my companions.

"We can not row, friend," say the crew; "there is not water enough; we are on the mud."

"The raft answers not the helm," says the pilot; "the mud is as thick as cement."

"Come this way, sirs, come this way," says the voice for a third time.

"Plunge the oars into the mud and push strongly," I say to my neighbors; "our lives depend upon your good will."

We all together push on the oars and begin to move slowly; some of us take oars and endeavor to row, (two men being at the same oar,) and we go quicker; we try to put up our sail, but it is useless—the wind is strong and the raft too heavy, being full of mud; we have water as high as the knees. We are obliged to manage our raft with the helm and the oars, and that exercise is very tiresome for men who have eaten almost nothing for sixty hours, who have had nothing to drink for more than two days, and who had not slept for three whole nights; but love of liberty holds up our courage and we are confident in God's mercy. We encourage one another and advance by degrees along the coast.

September 16th, 8 o'clock A. M.

We are in a sort of bay at the mouth of a river, which we suppose to be the Maroni river, that separates French Guiana from Dutch Guiana. The flood pushes our raft into the river and we endeavor to take ground on our right, (the left bank of the river,) where is a Dutch settlement.

Twelve o'clock. We land near some huts, and a white building supposed to be a Dutch dwelling. We have met in the river several canoes manned by Indians; we asked them, by signs, to give us provisions, but we didn't understand their answer and no provisions were given us.[24]

In approaching the huts we meet Indians, and inquire for food and drink once more. The Indians take what we give them in payment for provisions, but they give us nothing in exchange and fly into the woods. We find fresh water and drink eagerly. We go to the white house for the purpose of asking hospitality, but it is uninhabited. We fall to the ground, discouraged, half dead of distress, and we sleep.

The want of food awakes me and some of my companions; we go out, searching for provisions, and meet many savages.[25] I can not say they are indecently dressed, because they are not dressed at all; but their skin is painted red.[26] They refuse us provisions. We ask them, by signs, if there are any Dutch settlements in the neighborhood. They point with their fingers in several directions, and fly into the woods. Soon after we see canoes with Indians crossing the river and going to the French shore, which is about two miles distant. We don't think it prudent to stay longer in this place; it is preferable to search for a Dutch plantation, where we may find a better hospitality.

We awake our friends and march together along the bank of the Maroni, trusting to meet civilized men. It is about 4 o'clock in the afternoon, and there is low water. We walk without any accident until about eight or nine o'clock, when we begin to find the ground softer and sink into the mud; we go a little more to the right, but the ground is worse than it was before; it is impossible to go farther, and we must return whence we came. We resolve among us to go back, to embark again on our raft, and to try to ascend the river by water;—but the ground grows softer and softer, and finally becomes rather liquid. (The flood is the cause of it, di-

24 The "Indians" referred to in the following pages belong to the Kalina people. The Kalina are native to the northern coastal areas of South America. Today they are to be found in Venezuela, Guyana, Suriname, French Guiana, and Brazil. Stories of encounters with French prisoners on the run persist in oral tradition.

25 Paon uses several derogatory terms to refer to the Kalina, which contrast starkly with his otherwise universalist rhetoric.

26 The red paint is obtained from the seeds of a tropical plant known as roucou.

luting the mud on which we are walking.) Our position is far from being comfortable. We are exceedingly tired, hungry and sleepy, but love of life strengthens us and we continue our journey through the mud, in darkness, and often call one upon the other, to prevent the missing of any of us. The tallest man of the troop has mud to his knees, and he calls for Bivors assistance. Bivors is the shortest of us, but he is good hearted and most courageous; he runs in the direction in which he has heard the voice, but when he is near his companion he has mud to the girdle. Then he says to his comrade:

"You are twice as tall and three times as strong as I; please to help yourself and do as I do;" and Bivors, who is a clever fellow, pulls off his coat, throws it on the mud and walks upon it. His friend follows his good example, and both, the Giant and the Dwarf, are out of danger.

We go hobbling along, but we never stand together; we never join our feet; on the contrary, we make large paces to prevent our sinking, and at last we reach a solid ground. We drink fresh water for our supper, and afterwards count ourselves. Several are missing. We divide into two parties; one goes back in search of our missing brethren, and the other takes rest.

The discovering party finds one lying down and sleeping—they awake him and tell him to follow them; they meet another who is walking on his hands and knees, not having strength enough to stand up—they relieve him; they see two others arm in arm and ready to faint—they give them assistance and encourage them. All return to our head-quarters. They drink water, wash their faces, feel a little better, and take rest. During the time the other party is in search of the remainder of our missing companions.

At daylight we are all reunited and continue to go—the strongest helping the others—in the direction of our raft. She is still lying at the same place, but, alas! she has neither sail nor oars; the savage Indians have, during our absence, taken them and every thing which was on her. It is impossible for us to embark again, and we seem to have lost all hopes of escape.

September 17th, noon.

Bivors and I are in search of provisions, when we see many savages coming to us; they are armed with swords and arrows, and some have muskets, which leads us to suppose they have bad intentions towards us. Several are dressed with our own clothes, those we left in the mud. Their chief, or he who appears to be so, is dressed in a curious style; he wears a general's hat with a large feather over it, has an officer's coat with private's epaulets and red pantaloons, but he has no shoes. From these circumstances we suppose that they are coming from the place we left this morning, and that they have been there purposely to rob us, and perhaps to kill us. Then we fly to the white building; the savages pursue us, but fear lends us wings and they can not seize us. We give the alarm to our companions; all come out and form themselves in two ranks near the house. They have no arms, but seem determined to fight to the last drop of their blood. At this sight the savages stop; their ardor is calmed, and the chief says in bad French:

"Come to Mana,[27] the French port—come to Mana."

I answer him that we are unwilling to go there, that we desire to go to a Dutch port. "Bring us there and you shall be well rewarded," add I.

"Mana, Mana," says the chief, and all his followers repeat "Mana, Mana," brandishing their arms.

The moment is critical; we see some more savages, men, women and children, coming from the woods, and others coming in canoes from the French shore. I think that boldness is necessary to save us; then I run to the chief, seize the collar of his coat, shake him violently, and say:

"Mr. Monkey, we shall not go to Mana, and you shall direct us to the nearest Dutch port. We will reward you generously. If you refuse, you shall be punished severely; we belong to a powerful nation which will kill you, your wives, your fathers and your children."

Here I must interrupt Paon's narrative and make some brief reflections.

In the situation in which he and his companions were, Paon was obliged to tell the Indians what he did, but the truth is this: We, Socialists, have neither nation nor brethren to protect us. France is the place of our nativity, but that is a mere accident. France is not our mother—she is a mother-in-law for us. The French governmental press has proclaimed this: "We must not discuss with Socialists, we must kill them;"—and Louis Napoleon has followed the advice. We don't call such a nation a

27 Mana, in French Guiana, was established in 1828 by the Catholic missionary Anne-Marie Javouhey as a self-supporting colony of Africans, seized from illegal slave ships, whom Javouhey hoped to prepare for emancipation. By the mid-1850s it was administered by the French state.

Christian nation; we call it a nation of barbarians. Our brethren have been killed, are in prison, are among convicts, are banished, or are wandering about the world. We shall be considered as enemies by all the enemies of humanity, by all the oppressors of peoples. We shall be oppressed in all nations, except in the northern parts of the United States of America. There, perhaps people will remember that their ancestors of Massachusetts and Pennsylvania were poor pilgrims as we are; that they were exiled Puritans and exiled Quakers, who had fled from persecutors and persecutions in England and Germany. Those models of freedom will, perhaps, admit us in their Commonwealth; they will give us an asylum, protection, friendship, and honorable employment. This is all we want; the bread of charity would be too bitter for us—we could not digest it. Now I continue Paon's narrative.

I don't know what produces such a good effect—whether it is my shaking, my menace, or my promise of reward—but the Indian chief becomes more polite than before, and he says with a mild voice:

"Don't be so passionate, sir; I will not hurt you; there is in the neighborhood a Dutch settler named Mr. Kapler,[28] and two of his friends are here now. But tell me who you are; are you escaped convicts—are you Frenchmen?"

I foresee the Indian's stratagem; he wishes to know if we are not a prey for his cupidity; because the French Governor, having lost all honesty, gives a high premium for our arrest when we are outside the penitentiaries. In consequence of this knowledge, I answer the Indian:

"Son of the forest, I am acquainted with Mr. Kapler; he is a friend of ours; send for his two friends and they will tell you who we are."

An express is immediately sent to Mr. Kapler's friends, and a treaty of peace seems to be concluded between us and the savages. But that peace is as soon broken as a Buonaparte's oath is betrayed.

The canoes coming from the French shore are landed; the Indians who manned them run hastily to their chief and talk with him most vehemently. Cupidity shines in the Indians looks, and their leader tells us with a formidable voice:

"You must come to Mana; I know you now; they give so much a head

28 August Kappler was a German explorer and naturalist and the founder of the settlement of Albina in 1846. He was on good terms with both Indigenous peoples and Maroons. He left Suriname in 1879.

for you, and you are very numerous; your capture is a good fortune for me. Come to Mana, and make haste; I am anxious to taste the French brandy."

"You are quite mistaken, captain Feather," I reply; "the French Governor gives a good price for us when we are caught alive, it is true; but he gives nothing for our bodies when we are taken dead; and we prefer death to slavery. Besides that the Dutch Government will punish you as murderers if you kill us upon its territories. Then we have nobody to fear, neither you nor your followers; we will fight until death, so that you shall not take us alive, and you will lose the profits of your crime."

Inflamed to rage at these words, the Indian chief vociferates:

"I will massacre you to the last person if you don't come to Mana."

"We are not easy to intimidate, Mr. Savage; we shall not go to Mana."

"Then you shall die. Mana or death!"

"Dutch settlement or fight!"

"To death! to death!" cries the Indian, and he instantly runs among his followers.

Bivors and I return to our companions. The Indians make an infernal racket; warriors, women and children are singing, whistling and vociferating. We are quiet and silent, but we are determined to sell our lives at the highest price possible; we take our knives and we intend, at the first shot or arrow, to run all together against those of our enemies who are armed with muskets, and to disarm them if we can.

Harmony seems lost forever; but it is suddenly restored by the unexpected arrival of two black men. The oldest of them is decently dressed and looks honest.

"Who are you?" says he to us.

"We are French Socialists, escaped from Cayenne."

"Very well, sirs, I know you; you fought in the year 1848, for the abolition of slavery, and you co-operated to the downfall of that degrading institution. You are in safety here; you are as safe as in your own homes. Put your knives in your pockets and be quiet." Then, turning to the Indians, he says: "Down with your arms, friends, down with your arms; keep them for a better occasion; there are no enemies here." He afterwards takes the hand of his young companion and tells him: "My dear child, these men are the deliverers of our brethren in the French colonies; thank them for their honorable conduct; they have spent their blood for us."

The two negroes shake hands with us most heartily, and the oldest inquires what we wish for. We ask him for provisions and Mr. Kapler's protection.

"Have you any money?" says he.

"Yes, sir, we have."

"Please to give me some."

Our new friend procures provisions from the Indians, and sends his son to obtain canoes for our voyage to Mr. Kapler's residence. Soon after we receive plenty of provisions; we have in abundance fowls, plantains, cassava-bread and cachiri, (a sort of beer made by the Indians.) Chickens are quickly killed, picked, cooked and eaten. There are only the skins of the bananas lying on the ground, and the jars of cachiri are emptied. We feel a great deal better; our minds are easier and our bodies are strengthened.

The canoes being ready, we embark in them. Each canoe is managed by six vigorous paddles, and we ascend the river very fast. Soon after sunset we arrive at Mr. Kapler's settlement, near which is anchored an English schooner.

Mr. Kapler is a most distinguished gentleman, who speaks French as well as it is possible to speak it. He receives us very kindly, asks us many questions, and seems satisfied with our answers. He inquires if we have wounded or sick, and offers to send us his physician.

"No, sir, don't take that trouble," answers one of us. "We are much obliged to you for your kindness, but we decline your offer; we only want your cook's visit; now we prefer big loaves of bread to small pills."

"You are genuine Frenchmen, indeed," answers Mr. Kapler, with a friendly smile; "among the most imminent dangers you are already joking and laughing; but, notwithstanding that, you are witty, cheerful and courageous. You shall have the freedom of my house, and I hope you will that of heaven."

The worthy gentleman sends us much more than we could expect of the best hospitality; he sends us bread, meat, fruit, and some bottles of wine; also blankets, cushions, and the mattresses of his own bed.

"God bless you, Mr. Kapler! God bless you, your lady, your children, and the whole of your posterity!"

We take our supper, drink a drop of wine, smoke a pipe, and afterwards endeavor to prepare our beds. We are happier than we have been for the last eight years. We lie down, and a beneficent sleep is not long in closing our eyes; but we murmur yet, "God bless Mr. Kapler."

September 18th, morning.

The Dutch settlement in which we are is composed of about fifty souls, men, women and children, white and black. The former are Swiss and German emigrants; the latter are African or native slaves, but they are not treated as such; they are boarded, lodged and paid like the other settlers. All of them are well satisfied with their situation and much devoted to Mr. Kapler, who is a good, wise and impartial father for the whole colony, say they. He is their mayor, their judge, their vicar, their legislator and ruler in every thing. Peace and happiness seem to reign over this small community. Persons believing that black people are unable to work without being slaves, will do well to come here; they will see that black men are not lazier than white when they are well paid, well treated and well ruled. The opinion of those persons, if sincere, will be greatly modified.

There are two visitors at Mr. Kapler's; one is the captain of the English schooner anchored in the river, the other is the leader of a mighty tribe of Negroes called the Boss.[29] He is a man of respectable appearance and he is well educated, speaking French, English, Dutch and also the dialect of the natives.

The Boss have been formed by slaves escaped from Cayenne and from Surinam.[30] The fugitives collected in the neighborhood of the Maroni; when they were hunted by the French soldiers, they crossed the river and retired into Dutch territories, and vice versa when pursued by Dutch soldiers. When both parties (French and Dutch) combined their movements and their forces against them, the Boss went into the depth of the virgin forests, where their pursuers could not follow them. They easily lived in this country, having plenty of fruits on the trees the whole year, an abundance of fish in the river, and game in profusion in the woods.

They increased so much in number and in power, that the Dutch Government was alarmed at their neighborhood and sent an expedition against them. The Boss retreated into the woods, drew their enemies into an ambuscade, killed a great number of them, harassed the remainder in their retreat, and obliged them to go back to Surinam.

29 The term "Boss" is short for *Bos Negers* in Dutch, meaning "bush Negroes" in English. It refers to the six Maroon peoples of Suriname. The "leader" mentioned here likely belongs to the Ndyuka people.

30 The Maroons originate in Suriname, not French Guiana. Paon's historical account of the Maroons, derived from what Kappler told him, contains several inaccuracies.

Several other attempts to disperse them were made by the government of Surinam. Sometimes defeated, sometimes victorious, the Boss never could be destroyed; on the contrary, recruiting auxiliaries amongst the slaves of their enemies, they succeeded in damaging severely the Dutch plantations. On their side, having no possessions, they had nothing to lose. They finally proclaimed themselves independent and forced the Dutch government to recognize their independence. Then a treaty of peace was agreed upon between the masters and their late slaves and signed by both parties.

Mr. Kapler pays us a visit; he says he is quite willing to assist us and to give us every facility to go to Surinam.

"In my settlement you are under the protection of the Dutch flag, and, according to the laws of nations, you ought to be safe," observes he; "but I have no soldiers to defend your rights and mine; I have but a few pieces of small cannon and I could not defend you against a French man-of-war which should attempt to enslave you once more. Then I think it prudent for you to prosecute your voyage to Surinam; there are strong forts in the river and Dutch ships of war in the harbor of Paramaribo; the French will never dare to capture you in that place, and they would here. If that event took place, they would say that it was a mistake, that they thought you were common convicts and not political prisoners; that they intended neither to violate our territories, nor to insult our flag; the Dutch government would be satisfied with these explanations, and you would be kept in prison, more closely than before. Under the reign of Mr. Louis Napoleon Buonaparte rights are nothing without fixed bayonets to enforce them."

We assure Mr. Kapler that we are quite willing to follow his advice.

"The English schooner sails to-day," continues Mr. Kapler, "take passage in her, I am going to meet the captain and I will obtain, I hope, good accommodation for you."

Mr. Kapler leaves us for a short time and comes back again with the English captain.

"Captain," says Mr. Kapler, "these unfortunate men wish to go to Surinam; please to take them with you; I will supply them with provisions."

"And they will give me 600 francs (120 dollars) for their passage," roughly answers the Englishman.

"I don't know," replies Mr. Kapler, "if they are worth that sum."

Instantly we empty our pockets and give the whole of our money to Mr. Kapler; there are 320 francs (64 dollars).

"That is not enough," says the captain, "I must have 600 francs."

Mr. Kapler goes out and comes back with some money in his hands.

"Captain," says he, "there are 200 francs more; this is all I possess now, and that makes 520 francs (104 dollars)."

"I shall not take less than 600 francs."

"But remember, Captain, that these poor men were in prison for more than eight years; they have lost all they had; they have escaped through many dangers; they are not in safety here; at any minute a French man-of-war may arrive and summon me to deliver them into the hands of their enemies."

"I don't care about such things, Mr. Kapler; they must give me 600 francs for their passage, otherwise I shall not take them; I am not a philanthropist, I am a matter of fact man, a man of business, a man of money."

"Very well, captain, you can leave us," says our host with dignity.

"Then good-bye, Mr. Kapler."

"Good voyage, Captain."

"Good-bye, Mr. Money," says one of us.

"What did you say!" exclaims the captain with an angry voice.

"I said," fiercely answers our friend, rising and going close to the Englishman, "I said 'Good-bye, Mr. Money;' I was thinking something else, but I didn't say it to you."

"What a roughness in the heart, what a pride in the temper has that son of rapacious England!—That people are proud of their riches, proud of their numerous ships of war, proud of their dominion over half of the world. But thy reign is ended, modern Carthage, and in less than half a century thou shalt be but a poor, small island, inhabited by fishermen and smugglers," says Mr. Kapler, when the English captain was gone.

"You say this in the bitterness of your anger, Mr. Kapler, but that is not your real opinion. England is powerful, her government is strongly seated, sometimes dishonest, but always skilful. We think you go too far in the prophecy of her decadency."

"Not at all, my good friends; England is hated amidst all her dominions, from her ill treated sister Ireland to the extremities of her vast empire, to the East Indies—her subjects anxiously wait for a good occasion to break their slavery. And she has two dangerous enemies, powerful and formidable."

"Who are these enemies?"

"France and the United States. Frenchmen can not lose the remembrance of Waterloo, and are burning to take a bright revenge. Americans ardently desire the possession of the two Canadas[31] and Nova Scotia; and, besides, they are tired, exceedingly tired of meeting English ships and English merchants in the markets of the whole world."

"And which one is the most dangerous for England?"

"Both are dangerous for her; the Americans pull down the English trade by their persevering opposition, and the French, the day following a revolution at home, will crush England in their clenched hands, as easily as I can crush a walnut between my teeth. England will be a mouthful for a Revolutionist Government, who will write Waterloo on one side of its flag and St. Helena on the other; who will warrant liberty of religion to Ireland, civil liberty to Scotland, and equality of rights to English laborers. The battle of Waterloo was, for England, her battle of Trasimene—she soon will have her battle of Zama;[32] and the East Indies will be free, the Canadas and Nova Scotia will be independent States annexed to the United States; starving Ireland will have bread for her inhabitants, schools for her children, and alms houses for her old men; the straits of Gibraltar will return to its rightful owners, the Spaniards and the French. The Chinese will not be poisoned any longer with opium. Every one will be satisfied, every one will clap hands at the sight of that fall, and they will write with big letters, on the ruins of the haughty Albion: 'HERE WAS LONDON, THE MONSTROUS LEECH OF ALL NATIONS.'

"But we lose our time in chattering about this," continues Mr. Kapler, "and we have something better to do. You must go to Surinam, and go directly; I apprehend a bad visit for you; you must go away."

"How can we go, Mr. Kapler?—how can we go?"

"Let me tell you, friends; I have a large old boat; she is ill fitted, but you are mechanics, I know, and perhaps some of you are carpenters. I will lend you the boat, and give you tools and materials; repair her as well and as soon as you can, and go away. I will send with you two of my men as pilots; they will return me the boat."

We eagerly accept Mr. Kapler's proposal, and immediately proceed to

---

31 The Province of Canada, as it was then known, was made up of Canada West and Canada East.

32 The Battle of Lake Trasimene (217 BC) and the Battle of Zama (202 BC) were major battles of the Second Punic War, fought between Carthage and Rome. The first was a victory for the Carthaginian forces of Hannibal; the second was a defeat and marked the end of the war.

put the boat in a seaworthy state. The same day in the evening, at about 9 o'clock, we leave the honest Mr. Kapler; our boat is well provided and sound. We drop down the Maroni and stop near its mouth, passing the night among the same Indians who lately attempted to capture us; but this time we are kindly received and entertained by them.

At daybreak, the following day, we embark again. We cross the mouth of the Maroni, and, as we enter into the sea, perceive the French steamer coming in our way. We then run cautiously near the shore to prevent her dangerous approach. We have a Dutch flag on our boat, and a pass written and signed by Mr. Kapler.

The third day of sailing, the 21st of September, 1856, at 7 o'clock P. M., we land at Paramaribo, the capital of Dutch Guiana, on the river Surinam, which gives its name to the whole country. We are delighted—we are walking on a free land—we are saved! We inquire for an Inn, but there are gendarmes, soldiers and policemen in Paramaribo, and they are, perhaps, taller, stouter and more numerous than in Cayenne.

When shall we find a country without such a people! Those wretches ask us who we are, where we came from, where we are going; where are our passports, our chests, our trunks and our sleeping caps; what is our business, if we are tailors or shoemakers; what we intend to do; if we are married or bachelors; if we have or have not children; how many children we have; if our children are boys or girls; if we are Roman Catholics or Huguenots, Jews or Mahometans; if we drink brandy or gin, wine or beer; if we eat meat or fish; if we prefer hot to cold weather; and many other stupid questions.

We tell them to leave us alone with interrogatories, and to show us an Inn where we may live on moderate terms.

"You want an Inn and a cheap one," say they; "we can easily satisfy you; come with us. We will introduce you into a good one, a first rate one;—you will have nothing to pay for your board and lodging. Come to prison!"

"To prison!" we exclaim; "and what have we done to be sent there? what crime have we committed? We have just arrived."

"It is true you have done nothing wrong in this place, but you have, perhaps, done wrong things in other countries, and must go to prison."

"But if we have, perhaps, done wrong things in any other countries, let those countries punish their own offences; you ought not to interfere in these things."

"We don't care; come to prison and hold your tongue."

"We shall not go; we must speak to the magistrates. Are there any magistrates in this country?"

"To be sure, we have magistrates of all descriptions, and good ones; they are highly paid by us and duly appointed by the King of Holland, who resides six thousand miles from here, and who never honored the Colony with his presence; but come to prison and make haste."

"We want to speak to the magistrates."

"You shall speak to them to-morrow, or some other day, but come to prison; we have no time to spare, and the magistrates are in the same case."

"Your magistrates are handsomely paid, you said just now; then they must have time to speak to those who implore the protection of the laws."

"How obstinate you are! If every one were so, we should not have time enough to accomplish our duties. Come to prison."

"Let us converse with your magistrates first."

"We will send for them, but it is merely to satisfy your eccentric fancy; we know perfectly well what the magistrates will tell you—the same as we say, 'Go to prison first; you may plead afterwards.'"

The attorney-general arrives; he is a very polite and good natured man; he pities our sufferings, sympathises with our misfortunes, but he orders us to be put in prison.

"What did I tell you? Come to prison," says the commander of the Policemen; "but don't be afraid of the prison, you will be very comfortable there; you will have good board, a pleasant lodging and nothing to do, besides. You will enjoy yourselves."

"Execute your orders, Policeman, and stop your reflections."

We go to prison, and, notwithstanding our griefs, we sleep soundly until the morning.

Early in the forenoon they remove us to another part of the fortress. We are much astonished, and exceedingly pleased, by meeting, in our new residence, several of our companions who had left Devil's Island about six weeks before on a raft.—"They were lost among the mud, killed by savages or eaten by wild beasts," our guardians had said, seeming to pity their fate, and in the hope, we presume, of preventing any further attempt to escape.

We embrace one another with tears of happiness in our eyes, and with delighted hearts. We ask them by what miracle they are alive yet.

"We have escaped by a miracle, indeed," say they; "but, unhappily, we have lost two of our companions, Bochinsky, the Pole, and Pianori, the Italian."

"And how did they die?"

"In the mud to their breasts, eaten by crabs; when the Indians found them, they were warm yet, but inanimate; their souls were gone back to the mighty Creator; their eyes, their ears, their noses and their fingers had been eaten by the crabs, and their corpses were filled by those voracious animals."

Poor Bochinsky had been transported and sent to Cayenne because he was a Pole and a Republican. The unfortunate Pianori had a brother, who attempted Louis Napoleon's life and who was executed for that; when they asked him why he had made his attempt, he fiercely answered: "Because the French tyrant has killed my beloved mother, the Roman Republic."—When they asked him if he repented of his act, he said: "Not at all; if I were able to do it again, I would do it." He died as a martyr, without fainting and without romancing; the last words his mouth pronounced were these: "You cut off the head, but you don't cut the tail of the conspiracy; and the tail is longer than the head, much longer, indeed." His young brother was transported after his heroic death; he was transported and sent to Cayenne for no other reason than his consanguinity, which his persecutors would never recognize—he was called Sasaloni by his jailers.

Two more Italians have been in dark cells, at Royal Island, in the red castle, for more than three years; they cannot walk in the passage, no one is allowed to converse with them, and no body knows their names. And the French imperial newspapers dare to publish that there are no political prisoners in Cayenne!

The *Moniteur* published that all those,—amongst the Republican prisoners,—who would submit to the Emperor, should be immediately enlarged and quite free. The two Italians, alluded to, amongst many others, have submitted to Mr. Louis Napoleon Buonaparte. [We could, if necessary, tell the person's name who wrote down this submission.] Notwithstanding this, all are in prison yet and will be in prison for life.

Buonaparte! Buonaparte! God is tired of your crimes.—Modern Attila! you will be hung, without fail, and that will not be a vengeance of your enemies, it shall be a heavenly punishment.

We are much excited by the sad death of our two late companions, and we beg the living to tell us the particulars of their escape. They agree to our request and are about to commence their recital when the visit of the Governor of Surinam is announced to us.

"Foreigners," says the Governor, "you affirm that you are political refugees, and I believe what you say, but I may suppose you are escaped convicts; in the first case you ought to be free; in the second I must send you back to Cayenne, in execution of the treaties existing between France and Holland. I will send to-day, without fail, a steam ship to Cayenne; at her return you shall be released if you are really political refugees."

"We take notice of your promise, Governor."

"I give you my word of honor to liberate you when I shall have the proof that you were political prisoners."

Remember, Governor. Remember!

We are alone now, and our fellow prisoners tell us the brief account of their escape in the following manner:

"In the beginning of August last we left Devil's Island, seven in number, on a raft made with empty casks. We in a few days were in sight of the Maroni, and the want of provisions obliged us to land on the Dutch bank, where we purchased water, plantains and cassava bread from the Indians. Having sailed again, we saw in the open sea a steamship, when, fearing to be perceived and caught, we ran toward the shore. When the steamer was passed and out of sight we tried to go farther from the shore, but could not; and the following night at high water, were driven ashore in a place encumbered with trees.

"At the break of day we looked around and saw nothing near us but mud and trees; the water was far before, the land far behind. We attempted to walk over the mud, but it was not possible, the ground being too pliant and soft. It was not easy, either, to go to the water. We tried to jump on the trees, but they were too small and could not bear the weight of our bodies. We were obliged, therefore, to stay where we were, but we hoped, at the returning tide, to be able to sail again. We were deceived in our hopes; the water did not come to our raft, which had sunk many inches in the mud since our arrival; we had no more provisions—not a bit of bread, not a drop of water. We remained in that place for ten days, starving and devoured by clouds of mosquitoes, sinking deeper and deeper in the mud, enduring all the sufferings that man can endure."

"But you could not stay so long without eating?"

"The mud was filled with crabs; we ate them."

"And what did you drink?"

"We drank our own water."

"And how did you escape?"

"The courage of despair incited us; we had remarked that the water was coming, every tide, nearer and nearer the place where we stood. Then we made another raft, and on the eleventh day, the water being higher than before, we put to sea again; but we never could, though we endeavored many times, leave the neighborhood of the shore. Our raft was so badly fitted that we were obliged to take ground again, but this time we succeeded in reaching land, and walked into the woods, eating wild fruit, raw roots, leaves of trees, and whatever we found; but having, happily, fresh water at will. We sent two of our party, the strongest, as a vanguard to Surinam, and pursued our way.

"Bochinsky was exceedingly tired; his legs were scratched in many places, and, being unable to follow us, he stopped, saying:

"'Death for death, I will die here;' and he laid himself on the ground.

"'You shall not die alone,' said Pianori; 'I am young and strong, and I will save you or we will die together. Brethren,' added he, 'prosecute your journey; if you escape, avenge us.'

"Our exhortations, our prayers, could not change Pianori's determination—he remained with his friend.

"We walked and walked about, and finally arrived at a Dutch settlement. Our vanguard succeeded in reaching Surinam, and sent us a boat; and we arrived here much harassed and wounded, but feel better now.

"As to Bochinsky and Pianori, we begged the Dutch authorities to send in search of them. They hesitated at first, and finally sent a boat; but it was too late, most precious time having been lost by our wavering protectors. Two corpses were found in the mud, where we suppose they had gone to seek crabs for their food. Since our arrival here we have been in prison, and we think you will be treated likewise."

The narrative of our friends is ended; we admire their courage and perseverance, pity their sufferings, and deeply regret the loss of two of our best companions in captivity. We are now twenty-five French Republicans in the prisons of Surinam. The Governor has kept his promise by despatching a vessel to Cayenne purposely for us, and we hope to be delivered at her return, which must be soon. We have confidence in the Governor's word of honor.

The ship is coming back from Cayenne—she enters the harbor—she brings letters for the Governor; we shall be free at length, after more than eight years of confinement.

Alas! we reckoned without our host! We receive a message from the Governor, which is very nearly as follows:

"I was most anxious to keep the promise I made you, and orders were to be given to set you at liberty; but the slave holders of the colony inform me that their negroes are impatient of the yoke and willing to break it. In the neighboring colonies, Cayenne and Demerara, negroes are free, and ours, incited by the Boss, we suppose, are unwilling to be slaves any longer; they imperatively demand their freedom, and are resolved to obtain it by force, if it is otherwise impossible. They would have taken arms already if they had leaders; happily they have not, but you could be such. Your avowed opinions, your well known courage and boldness, your knowledge of arms and discipline, render you dangerous for the quietness of the colony. The slave owners beg me to keep you in prison, and I cannot refuse their request. I do not share in their fears; I have confidence in your common sense; I hope you would not interfere with our municipal laws, (and slavery is a municipal law,) but prudence compels me to confine you."

Your logic, Governor, is very curious indeed; it is as curious as your acts. When we arrived, you told us that being outlaws in other countries, we must be outlaws here. You then interfered in oppressors' injuries; you proclaimed, then, solidarity between law givers. You say now that we must not interfere in the grievances of the oppressed—then you condemn solidarity between the subjects of the law. You consequently disapprove today what you approved yesterday; you then approve or disapprove according to your interests. This may be adroit, but it is neither honest nor logical!

The above is our answer if you are an Apostle of Solidarity. If you are not such—if you proclaim the contrary—if you believe that a nation has not a right to interfere in another nation's affairs—that a community ought not to interfere in the affairs of others—that a man is quite free to do what he likes in his home—to manage his business as he thinks to be the best; we will beg your permission to answer you as follows:

The law of Solidarity is a natural law, and men (whoever they may be) cannot destroy it. People or Legislators may make laws against it, but these laws in many circumstances will not be followed with their authors' consent or against it; the exceptions will be as numerous as the cases where the rule is against the laws of nature. Examples: you have two neighboring nations bounded by a common river; each one has proclaimed that they can do at home what they like. Do you think that one of them has the right to turn aside the river from its natural bed, and by that means to deprive the other of water? Certainly not; nature has given the river to both of the territories—it belongs to both.

"My home is my castle," says a free citizen. According to the laws of men this may be right. According to the laws of nature, this is often wrong. If you are about to kill somebody in your home or set it on fire, I break open your door or your window, I enter your castle and I prevent you from killing or setting fire, every one will confess that I am a good citizen; I have saved a person from death or a town from incendiarism. No law can punish me for that.

Consequently your liberty ends where the liberty of others commences. Consequently every one has a right,—more than a right, a duty,—to prevent what may hurt others' interests, persons or property. Slavery is in that case, because slavery injures all human creatures.

Nature or God,—as you like,—has made all men equal in rights at their birth; no one is or can be the property of another. If you make man property, you go against the laws of nature, you insult God, you cease to be a man, you become a Satan—a rebellious angel. Man has a three fold life; he lives physically, morally and intellectually. By slavery you kill both his moral and intellectual life; you, then, kill two thirds of him; you destroy God's work. And you dare to call yourself a Christian! What a folly!

You say that we must not interfere in the question of slavery? But a negro is a man as well as you and I; he is a member of humanity. Consequently, when you abase him you abase me, and you abase yourself. When you kill his mind and his dignity, you kill a part of mine and of yours, because you hurt a member of the community which we belong to. You say: "Let every one, nation, province, city or citizen, manage the affairs of their interior; you have nothing to do with them."

For things concerning you and you alone, I am willing to do it, but for slavery I am not, because my duty, my imperious duty, tells me to interfere. If I hurt your nose with my hand, yours, probably, will strike me in the face. Vainly I will tell you that your hand having not been injured, had not a right to interfere in the contest between mine and your nose; you will rightly answer that a part of your person having been offended, the whole of your body is offended and delegates, for revenging, the part of it which is the best fitted for doing so. You will be right, perfectly right, and so I am when I say: "Negroes are men like me; they belong to Humanity and who insults, offends, injures, abuses, kills part or whole of them, insults, offends, injures, abuses or kills me."

Some persons believe that the climate of some countries render slavery absolutely necessary, because the whites cannot work in those countries and the blacks would not, if free, work for the whites. We don't know if that opinion is right or wrong, but, in both cases, that is not a reason to make blacks slaves. If negroes went to Northern countries and say to the inhabitants: "It is too cold for us here, we are unable to get our living by our own work, please to work for us, be our slaves;"—the Northmen would probably answer: "Go to the South, if you like, but we shall not work for you, we refuse the honor to be your slaves."

Some others pretend that the darkness of the skin proves a low intelligence and fatally designs the negroes to slavery; but if that is true, whiter is the skin, broader is the mind, and, consequently, the red haired men ought to make every one else slaves.

Every reason given by the apostles of slavery is worse the one than the other. There is but one right to make men slaves—that invocated by the wolf wishing to eat the lamb, the right of the strongest.

Governor of Surinam, be free once in your life—once is not custom— confess that and let us tell you this:

"Our small ability, our hands, our heads, the whole of our person, are devoted to the oppressed willing to break their yoke; everywhere, at any moment, we will be ready to pursue our mission, to abolish the shameful institution called slavery."

The effects of that institution are worse, perhaps, for the masters than for the slaves; it renders them corrupted, ignorant, lazy and cruel.

"And now also the axe is laid unto the root of the trees: therefore every tree which bringeth not forth good fruit is hewn down, and cast into the fire." [Matthew, chap. III.]

In all ages, and among all nations, the oppressors have the same tactics; having no good reasons to give to their opponents, they decline any discussion and proceed by violence. Prometheus is nailed on a rock; Socrates is poisoned; the divine Jesus is crucified; Christians are devoured by lions and tigers; Galileo is confined; Huguenots are massacred in France; John Huss is burnt in Bohemia; Quakers and Puritans are banished from England. But, notwithstanding calumnies, auto-dafe, banishment, tormentors and scaffold, all progresses were, are, and will be fulfilled. The light of Prometheus prevails over the darkness of ignorance; the unity of God is agreed; Christianity rises radiantly and drives out the Pagan gods; the earth is round and moving, instead of being flat and still; the Reformation is proclaimed and accepted. Every step in the progress of humanity is indicated by a large stream of blood; every progress must have its persecutors, its martyrs and its avengers; Socialism is in these conditions, and, if it is in want of something, it is not of martyrs.

We were put in prison under Gen. Cavaignac's government, by the ignorance of the French Republicans, because we foresaw, before they did, the abyss into which our freedom was to be precipitated. Louis Napoleon Buonaparte was then neither Emperor nor President, member of the National Assembly, nor French citizen; he was nothing more, nothing less, than a citizen of Thurgovy, Switzerland.[33] He kept us in prison, when elected President, by want of dominion, and when he was proclaimed Emperor he made a compromise with the faithful followers of Henry the Fifth;[34] the death of Socialism was the price of their adhesion to his government. We receive now the kick of the ass;[35] slaveholders confine us for want of money, slavery having no other right than force and no other purpose than money making. Slaveholders, you are men of money; you would do everything for money, and it is very lucky indeed that the sun is so far from your crooked hands and so difficult to catch; otherwise you would take it, saying that God made it for you alone, as you are not ashamed to say that God permits slavery; you would take the sun, share it amongst you, put your part in your deepest pockets, and we, poor disgraced men, would be obliged to stay in eternal darkness, or to purchase light of you. You always say, "Slavery is a very fine institution; hurrah for Slavery!" But if so, if it is so good, taste a little of it; act as you speak and

---

33 Louis-Napoleon spent part of his youth in Switzerland. In 1832 he was made an honorary citizen of the canton of Thurgau (*Thurgovie* in French).

34 Henri, Count of Chambord, grandson of Charles X, was the Legitimist pretender to the French throne under the name of Henri V.

35 The French phrase *le coup de pied de l'âne*, here translated literally, describes an attack on an already defenseless opponent.

be slaves for a while. After a few months of experience, if you are satisfied with your condition, if you consent to be slaves forever, I promise you to follow your example; my friends and I will make ourselves slaves forever. Otherwise, if you refuse, I will call you the greatest charlatans in the world, which is so filled with charlatans!

Against slaveholders, oppressors and speculators of all kinds, names and descriptions, Socialism will fulfill its work, which is abolition of slavery, of whatever degree it may be, in every country where it may exist, by whatever name it may be called. Its apostles are dispersed over the four quarters of the world, but they are confident in the truth of their principles, and they have the sympathies of all men of faith and honesty. They will succeed in their endeavors.

We stay in the prisons of Surinam for two months. Half of us are already gone away when the Governor resolves to send us to Georgetown. We go on board the Dutch mail steamer. Paramaribo seems to be a clean and handsome town, the streets of which are covered with fine yellow sand, and there is no dust nor ashes in them.

We arrive at Georgetown; we have no money, no clothes, no acquaintances, and are unable to speak a single word of English. The Dutch bring us ashore and leave us to God's care. What must we do? what will become of us? The inhabitants look at us as at most curious animals; we don't understand them, they don't understand us. A black man once more is our deliverer; he brings us to the Governor's palace. We wait a couple of hours, and his Excellency at last comes with his Secretary. We tell them our position.

"I have spent much money for your companions," says the Governor; "I paid their passage to the United States, I bought them clothes and shoes, and I paid their board and lodging in Georgetown until they left it. I can do no more; but if you are willing to work, I will give you employment. Do you accept?"

"Yes, sir, we do; we will be much pleased to get our living by our own work. We are fatigued and feeble, but we will do our best."

"Very well; take this letter and go to the fort; you shall have work and 80 cents per day."

From Demerara to Boston

Paon's manuscript is ended here. I have translated it almost literally. I could have made several changes by supposing some things and adding some others; but I preferred to give it as I received it. Its reading plunges me into deep reflections, and I exclaim:

"A cause that possesses such soldiers cannot perish, and Socialism shall not perish; no, no, that is impossible!"

But my friends can not stay here any longer; the greater part of them have left Georgetown and gone to England or the States; there remain only five. I would take with me the whole of them, but I am too poor for that. I left Cayenne precipitately, and left the little I possessed. They owed me some money, but I had no time to cash it. Besides, I am almost naked; I must buy clothes and linen from the feet to the head. Nevertheless, I will take with me Paon and Bivors. "What is sufficient for one is sufficient for two," says the French proverb; and with good will, I add, may be sufficient for three.

I am advised that a Salem vessel is at Surinam now, and I am convinced that her captain, who is an acquaintance of mine and a perfect gentleman, will not refuse to take us free of any charge for our passage. I then write a letter to the Governor of Demerara, purposely to beg of him our free passage for Paramaribo; and I write another letter to my best friend in Cayenne, whom I empower to cash for my account the money due to me in that town, and I tell him to send it to me as soon as possible.

Paon is at the Colonial Hospital, severely wounded. I ask Bivors if he is willing to follow me to the United States of America.

"It is my earnest desire," says Bivors; "I am tired of Georgetown; its climate is too unhealthy for Europeans, and its inhabitants are too much corrupted for honest people; but I have not sufficient money to pay my passage. I arrived here eight months ago, and with the greatest economy I have saved, since my arrival until now, but a few dollars, having been sick many times, and living being very dear here."

"Don't mention it, Bivors, my good friend; I have some money; I shall receive some more by and by; we will share the good as well as the bad fortune."

We are told that Governor Woodhouse leaves Georgetown to-day; I am anxious to be present at his departure, because opinions differ respecting his character; many flatter him, and many others despise his conduct. I go with Bivors to see the ceremony of his sailing to Europe. We arrive at the public buildings; the square is crowded with soldiers, policemen, and people of all colors, from the deepest black to the faintest white. The mob seem very impatient to see their beloved Governor, and more impatient to wish him a good farewell.

The folding doors are solemnly opened at the buildings, and Governor Woodhouse appears at the threshold of the door in all his majesty, followed by a multitude of lackeys. Drums are immediately beaten, and public functionaries applaud loudly; but the mob roar energetically in expression of their dissatisfaction and contempt. The Governor, with a disdainful shrug, then advances arm in arm with his lady upon one side, and the bishop on the other, surrounded by his high officers; the soldiers' band plays *God save the Queen*, and the procession continues its way amongst the thickest ranks of the people. Some individuals throw at Governor Woodhouse and his staff, sweet potatoes, plantains, oranges, and other fruits and vegetables; the Governor laughs loudly, and his officers follow his example; the band plays *Rule Britannia*, and they continue their way, making gestures of deep disgust, of supreme arrogance. The mob, indignant, take dirt and stones and throw them at their Chief Magistrate.

Mr. Woodhouse is not laughing now, but becomes as pale as a corpse; soldiers are under arms, policemen on foot and on horseback are present, all of whom contemplate the scene, but no one moves; no one helps the mob, but no one prevents them from stoning the Governor. Mr. Woodhouse is wounded on the head and bleeding; his lady is fainting; and the Bishop is almost dead with terror. The pride of the Governor and his staff being driven out, the mob becomes suddenly as quiet as before; every one returns to his home or to his business without making the least noise, without the least appearance of anger. I am amazed at that strange uproar, and I ask Bivors what are the causes of such an extraordinary thing.

"The only cause," says Bivors, "is an unjust tax, ordered by the Governor last year. Unjust causes always produce bad effects. You have seen the disorder; if, unhappily, soldiers or policemen had attempted to prevent it, Georgetown would be now in open insurrection, and blood would be running in the streets. All that is by the Governor's fault."

"Tell me the reason of it, if you please."

"I will. About one year ago—I was not here then—a conflict took place between the colored working men of Georgetown and the Portuguese, emigrants, because the latter used to work for a cheaper price than the former. The black men and the mulattoes assaulted the Portuguese who fled instantly, leaving their work and their shops, and some disorder ensued. Sausages, hams, and bottles of liquor were destroyed—drunk and eaten, I must say,—by the black warriors, and their bones or empty bodies laid down on the field of battle. The garrison, composed of black men, were unable to restore harmony between the two camps; then French soldiers were required by the English Government and sent by the Governor of Cayenne. At their approach the blessings of peace arose once more over the colony.

"Governor Woodhouse, under those circumstances, took openly the part of the Portuguese; he estimated their losses according to their own valuation, and paid them without making any investigations. Whoever knows the rapacity and bad faith of the vile Portuguese, is certain that they received three times more than they had lost in the riot.

"The Governor went farther. For the purpose of recovering the amount of the damages, he decreed a uniform and general tax upon the inhabitants of the colony; rich or poor, black, colored or white, married or single, man or woman, every one had the same sum to pay. For the rich merchants or the wealthy ship-owners, capitalists or office holders, the tax was a trifle; but for the poor mechanic out of employment it was a heavy charge and many were unable to pay. The Governor ordered a fine and increased the expenses against them. Being unable at first, to pay two dollars, they could not pay six. Mr. Woodhouse sent them to prison. The jails of Georgetown were filled, then, with girls, women and old men; many died of despair and ill-treatment in their dull cells, and the others are in prison yet. You have seen the friends and relations of the victims wishing a farewell to their beloved Governor."

I have occasion to meet an old aristocratic lady, a sort of doll, handsomely dressed, making grimaces when smiling, rolling her eyes, as a dying cat, when speaking. I ask her opinion about the late event.

"Governor Woodhouse is a most perfect gentleman," says she, "he is the best administrator we ever had or ever can have; the mob who have insulted and assaulted him are exclusively composed of low people, ancient slaves, beggars-like, badly educated; they are thieves and murderers, and it is a shame for us not to kill them to the last one."

I take leave of the charitable old lady, and, soon after, I meet several ship captains of my acquaintance, and ask them the same question. They unanimously answer me:

"Governor Woodhouse had but half of what he deserves; he is a violent, haughty and unjust man, a stony-hearted, iron-headed man."

"But, Captain, he had his lady with him."

"His lady is worse than himself."

"But the Bishop has been wounded too."

"The Bishop is worse than either."

After my inquiries I know a little less than I did before. I return with Bivors to Paon's room, and find newspapers on the table. I read them, and I see the account of a dreadful insurrection in the East Indies, among the native soldiers. English men have been massacred, and the insurgents are numerous, disciplined, well armed, and disposed to fight to the death.[36]

"Ah me!" I say, "it appears that Mr. Kapler was not so wrong as I thought at first; this is the first wave of the returning tide against England's dominion; I begin to believe that she will become lower than she became high."

I have been in Georgetown for a fortnight, and have had time to make myself acquainted with the country and its inhabitants. Demerara is richer and better cultivated than Cayenne; it produces much sugar and molasses, of which a great part is exported to the United States; its rum is of good quality; it possesses steam engines, and a railroad crosses part of the country toward Berbice. The harbor of Georgetown is very spacious

36 The Indian Rebellion of 1857 saw Muslim and Hindu soldiers (or sepoys) rise up against their British officers. The mutiny led to a mass revolt against British rule.

and many ships lie in it; handsome wharves allow vessels to land their cargoes and to load without loss of time and money; lights are placed at the entrance of the river to prevent shipwrecks; business is very active and profitable.

Nothing like this exists in Cayenne; there is no produce but a very small quantity of sugar and roucou; no wharves for ships—they load and discharge their cargoes by means of lighters; no roads in the country, except a sort of narrow way; it is so badly cultivated, so poorly inhabited, that large tigers are killed at broad day-light in the middle of the town. I saw the corpse of one of these wild animals which had been shot by a soldier in a house opposite the jail. Its numerous magistrates and office holders are anxious for nothing but to fill their purses with stolen gold; its innumerable policemen fill their stomachs with adulterated liquors.

As to corruption of manners, Demerara is worse, if possible, than Cayenne; the whole day you can see drunkards staggering, quarreling and fighting every where, particularly in the public houses, where Portuguese are selling, at high prices, different sorts of grossly poisoned liquors with pompous names, as: splendid rum, rich cordial gin, best genuine old cognac brandy. The whole night, principally on Saturdays, the streets are crowded with females of all countries, of all colors, of all conditions, smiling significantly to every one, but, above all, to those who seem to have money in their pockets. Cayenne and Georgetown are sisters in corruption, as were Sodom and Gomorrah.

I have paid a visit to Capt. Foskey on his ship. A French steam man-of-war was alongside the Chevalier; she was in want of fifty tons of coal. As no one among the English crew could speak French, and nobody among the French could speak English, mate Tutton asked me to be his interpreter. I accepted, and delivered the coal to the French ship. When this had been done, a master asked me if I was not a political prisoner escaped from Cayenne.

"Yes, sir, I am," said I.

"How did you manage your escape?"

"As I could."

"What ship brought you here?"

"I don't remember."

"Don't you fear to be captured here?"

"No."

I have received an answer from the new Governor, Mr. Walker; I have not had the honor to be received by him—he is too high and I too low—but his Secretary, Mr. Goodman, told me that his Excellency was willing to give a free passage to Surinam to three of us. I thanked him, and hoped to be able to prosecute my way to the United States in company with Paon and Bivors.

I had news from my friend in Cayenne; he sent me a kind letter and some money. I thought I was certain to leave English Guiana. I went to the colonial hospital, inquired for the doctor, and asked him if it was possible to remove Paon without any serious danger.

"With a good bandage and some precautions he can make the voyage," said the physician.

I then inquired for the captain of the Dutch mail packet.

"Captain, I am your most devoted servant."

"Good morning, sir; how can I oblige you?"

"By carrying me and two of my friends from here to Surinam."

"Who are you, sir?"

"A political refugee, captain."

"What countryman are you?"

"French."

"I can not do what you require."

"Will you be so kind as to tell me why not?"

"Because I have strict orders not to bring any French refugees into the Dutch possessions."

"But we don't intend to go into Paramaribo; we will stay in the harbor, on board the brig Frederic, until she starts for Salem."

"Well, sir, I will ask the Governor of Surinam. If he allows me to take you, I will do it with the greatest pleasure on my next voyage."

"But, Captain, the Frederic will be gone then."

"I can not help it; I must execute the orders I have received. If you were in Surinam, I could take you here; but from here to Surinam I can not. I am sorry for it, but it is quite impossible for me."

"But our passage will be paid, Captain—well paid."

"Never mind; I can not take you at any price."

Farewell to my hopes of going to the United States by that way. I must look for another.

I inquired for American ships; there were none in the harbor of

Georgetown. Now I spend money every day and receive none; Paon is wounded and Bivors is sick; he has a bad cold and a worse fever; he lies on his bed. What shall we do, good God?—what shall we do?

Captain Foskey is in want of a cook; I promise him to inquire for one. Bivors feels better, and begs to be Capt. Foskey's cook.

"We have but little money," says he; "keep it for Paon and you; I will go to England, and thence I will try to be shipped for the States. I will there join you and will have some money, and that is a good thing in many circumstances."

I send Bivors to Capt. Foskey early in the morning, and about ten o'clock I go to see how he manages his cooking. I find him much troubled; he can not make himself understood, and the steward, when he asks for black pepper, gives him white salt. Capt. Foskey, having invited two of his friends to breakfast with him, is displeased with the *debut* of his French cook, having bought a fine looking on kidney and the best beef steaks he could find, and nothing being ready in time. I immediately ask for all necessary things, cook the Captain's breakfast, and partake of it with them. The company are well satisfied with my cooking, and Capt. Foskey tries to induce me, once more, to go with him; he offers me four pounds sterling per month to become his cook. I tell him I can not accept. One of his friends offers me five pounds. I answer that my refusal is not a question of money.

"Why, then, are you so hard with us? do you hate English people?"

"No, Captain, no; I hate nobody in the world. My heart is so filled with love that there is no room for anger in it. I don't hate Englishmen as individuals; on the contrary they are good, and I like them very much. I travelled, in my youth, through all England for four years, and I was kindly received in every part. But I don't like the English Government."

"Why so? The English are a free people."

"They are, indeed; they are as free as oxen tied to the yoke; they are free on the condition of spending their sweat for the feeding of their fat oligarchy and their fatter monarchy."

"But in the United States it is the same under another name. Every where there are rich people and poor ones. The form of the Government in a country makes no difference."

"I beg your pardon, Captain; the form of government is all for freedom. In the United States, you say, they are as wrong as in England; but that, if true, proves nothing; people there elect their magistrates, from the President of the Republic to the modest town selectmen. Having the right to elect them, they have the right to dismiss them when they act wrong.—People make laws themselves, and are interested to make them good. Laws in that country will become better and better, and they will finally be perfect, whilst in England you will be proud slaves until the last judgment."

"What do you intend to do, when in the United States?"

"I will refute the calumnies told and written against Socialists."

"But that is done; we know, now, that Socialists don't deserve the bad fame they have had."

"You know nothing about it, Captain, and I will give you a proof of what I say. I find in your best dictionary the following description of Socialism: '*Socialism*. A social state in which there is a community of property among all the citizens; a new term for Agrarianism. [See Communism.]' The decision is quite wrong. Socialism and Communism are two distinct things. In my name, in the name of the party I belong to, I protest against it. Socialism, or social science, is a new science having for its purpose to seek the best means of securing to all citizens of the commonwealth the greatest portion of comfort, knowledge, freedom—of *happiness*, in one word. This is what we call Socialism; but Bonaparte, the perfidious, calls it by another name, and his allies do as he does."

"I find you in fault. You said just now that you hated nobody, and you hate the Emperor of the French."

"You are mistaken again, Captain; I don't hate Louis Napoleon Buonaparte, I only pity and despise him. I pity him because, having the power to become a Washington, the father of his country, he has preferred to be a Napoleon—a killer of men—What a pity! I despise him for the death of his brother, in Italy, at the fight of Forli; I despise him for his attempts at Strasburg and Boulogne; I despise him for his conduct in England, in the U. States, in France; I despise him for his ingratitude and bad faith; I despise him for his treacherous calumnies against us; I despise him, above all, because he tried, by every means, to abase his victims. What a shame! Louis Napoleon Buonaparte is a —— fool; he had me in his power for nine years, and he didn't kill me! I owe him the justice to say he tried many times, but he never could. I have a strong will, be assured. I was willing to live and I lived. Do you know, captain, what I will do, when in the United States? I bring with me part of the irons I wore in St. Joseph Island. Paon is a blacksmith—he will make the rest, he will make the instruments of torture we had; I will acquire a good mastery of the English language, and, afterwards, I will go from city to city, from town to town, from village to village, making public every where and exhibiting to every one the ill-treatment we suffered—we, honest men, a thousand times more honest than Mr. Louis Napoleon Buonaparte and his followers. You don't know who I am, sycophant of sycophants; you don't know what I can do; I am not of those who kill monarchs, but I belong to those who render monarchies impossible; you tried to kill us, poor dwarf, but we are hydra-headed, we are invulnerable as a party. You lose your time and the few brains that the mighty Creator put into your bald head."

The 14th of August Bivors tells me there are two vessels for America in the harbor; one of them is a Yankee and the other is English. I begin with the Yankee and I meet the captain, who is a Swede—he wants fifty dollars for each of us, leaves Georgetown in about two days and goes to New York. The passage is too dear, his departure too late, and New York is not the place where I wish to go. I meet the English captain, who is a Portuguese under the name of a New England seaman; he agrees to take us three for ninety dollars, and he starts in two days. I accept the bargain, give him his money and take leave.

Mr. Goodman, the Governor's Secretary, meets me in the street, and asks me what I intend to do; I tell him I am to leave Georgetown after to-morrow.

"Have you sufficient money for your passage?"

"I have paid it, but we are in want of warm clothes, so useful in cold countries."

"Come to-morrow to the Governor's dwelling, at one o'clock."

"I will come, sir."

The next day, at one o'clock P. M., I meet Mr. Goodman.

"The Governor is satisfied with you; here is an order on the Treasurer-General of the Colony; he will give you fifty dollars and I wish you a good voyage."

"I thank you, sir, in my own behalf and that of my friends," I say to Mr. Goodman, and I add between my teeth: "If all the Governors of the English possessions were like Mr. Walker, England's dominion would last a little longer."

We buy the indispensable things for our voyage and we make our adieus to our acquaintances. One of our countrymen is to marry, in a few days, a fair young lady; I wish them concord and happiness.

We pay the small debts we had in Georgetown, pack our trunks and on Sunday morning, the 16th of August, 1857, we embark on board the Sylph, going to Boston via Turk's Island.

We leave Georgetown on Sunday afternoon; mate Tutton comes on board the Sylph in company with another mate; both give the best references about us to the Captain, to the mates and to the owner of the vessel, a Portuguese of Madeira. There are two passengers besides us; one is a young doctor and the other is the keeper of the Ice House of Georgetown; the former is travelling, and the latter, a Portuguese, goes to Boston to obtain ice and provisions for his hotel. The first mate is a native of New Jersey, and speaks French as a real Frenchman; the crew is entirely composed of colored men and the cook is as black as a coal.

At about six o'clock the owner of the vessel pays me a visit.

"Sir," says he, "you paid me your passages that is true, but among the money you gave me were English pieces for a value of thirty dollars, and the American dollar is worth one hundred and four English cents; therefore, you owed me thirty times four cents."

"And that makes?" I say.

The Portuguese counts on his fingers, and, after some minutes, says:

"That makes one dollar and forty cents."

"You are wrong, Sir," I tell him with a smile; "that makes only one hundred and twenty cents; you are a good merchant, but a bad arithmetician."

"O! dear me, sir, I wouldn't cheat you, that makes one hundred and forty cents; but I sympathize with your misfortunes and two honest seamen recommended you to me; therefore, I will accept one hundred and thirty cents."

"I will give you nothing at all, master thief; I have no money; spent all I had."

"Oh, no, sir, you wouldn't deceive a poor man, who is the only support of his wife and his large family, besides his father, his mother and two uncles. Good sir, you look honest, you seem to be a gentleman; you wouldn't keep the bread and the sweat of poor people; give me one dollar and twenty cents and I acquit you."

"Here is your money."

"I thank you, Sir; I am much obliged to you; God bless you and your two companions; all three of you seem to be good natured men; you will not refuse to lend a hand to the crew; these poor fellows have a hard labor;

they are only five instead of eight, and you can help them; one of you will help the cook and the two others can help the crew for the manœuvres; that will be an amusement for you, time is so long on a sea-passage!"

"Mr. Portuguese," I tell him, "my companions are unable to work; Paon is wounded and Bivors feels sick; and for myself, if I was willing to be your cook, instead of giving you money for my passage, I would receive some of you; but, never mind, we will help your men when we please!"

"That is all right, sir, you are a first rate gentleman," says the Portuguese, and he carefully puts his money in a leather purse, ties it many times, puts it in an inside pocket cautiously, wraps his kerchief over it and caresses the whole with delight.

"Now, Mr. Portuguese, where shall we sleep?"

"I don't know, sir, I have no beds, but I can give you mine and sleep on the sofa."

"And my friends?"

"They will find a place, they are skilful; they soon will find a comfortable bed room and make a nice bedstead."

The weather is beautiful and I sleep on deck this night. The next day at sunset, I tell the Portuguese I will take his bed.

"Dear sir," says he, "I can't give it to you because I gave it to my countryman, the passenger."

"Well, sir, then I will sleep on the sofa."

"You can't, sir; I gave it to the good doctor."

"Where shall I sleep, then?"

"Where you like, sir; I put my ship at your disposal. The chief cabin is full, the forecastle is too narrow for the crew, the stem is encumbered with mud and stones, but you can sleep any where else; I don't care, I am too honest a man to refuse you a bed and a bedstead if I had any, but I have not, unhappily. Do for the best, my good sir, do for the best; our voyage can't be long—a few days are soon past."

"From head to foot, Mr. Portuguese, you are a blackguard."

"Oh! dear Sir, I assure you—"

"Silence! if you speak to me again, I will answer you with my shoe."

The cook is a youth quite unacquainted with cooking; he is steward, besides, and required very often to assist the crew; he is shipped at the rate of eight dollars per month. We help that unfortunate. The Portu-

guese strikes the poor boy; we tell the Portuguese to do it no more, otherwise he will be fined when the ship arrives at Boston.

After nine days of sailing we arrived at Turk's Island, and find three
Boston vessels there. Paon, Bivors and I land, purposely to beg our passage on board of one of them, but we cannot meet their captains and the
next day they start. We are obliged to pursue our voyage in the Sylph.
Turk's Island is a British possession, a most desolate land, producing only
salt, sand and rocks. Nothing can grow there; there are neither trees nor
grass—the earth is quite naked. The inhabitants are almost savages, and a
foreigner, for them, is an object of curiosity.

We leave Turk's Island, and our condition becomes worse and worse;
the bread is spoiled and filled with worms; the flour has been finished for
two or three days, and potatoes are unknown on board the Sylph. Passengers and sailors are much dissatisfied, but the Portuguese is delighted; he
will make plenty of money with the salt he has bought, and he has already
made some with his passengers. In a few years he will be a rich man and
he will say:—"I had much trouble to make my fortune." I think it would
be more proper to say: "I starved many men in making my fortune."

The mate is fishing; he catches two enormous fishes.

"All right," says the Portuguese, "we will cook one for our dinner and
I will salt the other for to-morrow."

"You can dispose of one, answers the mate, but I have disposed of the
other; it belongs to the Frenchmen who have nothing else to eat."

Immediately Bivors takes one fish and he chooses the biggest; the Portuguese looks piteously, but he dares not say a word.

We have a dead calm for six days, during which the two Portuguese
play cards. They play a curious game: the winner drinks ale or brandy and
the other nothing, but he pays the value of the liquors. The sailors send
towards the players angry looks and say: "It is bad to play cards on board
a ship; we shall have no wind for a long while."

In the Gulf of Florida we have a violent storm; the wind is so furious
and the sea so rough that we must clue up all sail, except the mizzen and
the fore. All hands are required for this manœuvre—crew and passengers.
The two Portuguese are pulling the ropes with me:—we have two feet of
water on the deck. The passenger asks me if I ever saw such bad weather
in my life.

"Yes, sir," I answer gravely; "I have seen two storms like this, but every time we threw the cargo into the sea and I think it would be prudent to do the same, now."

"Indeed!" says the owner, "but my cargo is not insured; if I lose it I am quite ruined; my cargo is as precious as my life."

"More precious, perhaps, but our lives are more precious than your salt."

The two Portuguese go to the cabin and cry like children; one is fearing for his salt, the other for his money, and both for their lives. During three whole days and three whole nights we have dreadful weather, and, afterwards, a calm again. Having nothing else to do, I play cards with Paon. The second mate tells us it is a shame to play cards on Sundays and particularly on board of ships. Paon raises his head, looks at him and sees his own knife in his hands.

"Mr. Preacher," says Paon, "I think it is worse to steal knives than to play cards; this knife is mine and I take it back."

We have a fair breeze and we think to be in Boston in two days. The Portuguese sends us the captain to take our names and to get six dollars for the head-tax imposed upon passengers coming to the United States. I have but English money and I pay the captain with that; but he soon comes back again and tells me the owner is not willing to take English shillings for more than twenty American cents.

"Very well, captain, give me the English money; I will give you American dollars."

"Here it is, sir."

"Tell the owner I will pay the head-tax myself," and I put the money in my pocket.

The 19th of September, 1857, at the break of day, we perceive Boston. This sight excites us as much as that of the promised land did the children of Israel, and we stay on deck, with our eyes fixed on the gigantic city. At ten o'clock we landed opposite the Custom House. We instantly uncover our heads and we exclaim with enthusiasm:

All Hail! land of the United States, land of freedom, land of the future, Hail! Country of Washington, whose immortal glory shines brighter and brighter every day, amongst all nations, and eclipses the false glory of the Alexanders, the Cæsars, the Napoleons! These great murderers were prodigal of men, caused streams of painful tears, and deserved the abhorrence of many peoples; Washington was economical of men, caused but tears of joy, and deserved the wonder of the world and of posterity.

Hail! State of Massachusetts, of which the sacrifices, in soldiers and money, contributed so much to the independence of the thirteen primitive States!

Hail! City of Boston, which, first among all cities, took arms against the oppressors!

Hail! Breed's hill,[37] glorious witness of the American citizens' bravery!

We pay the head-tax, we take the railway and we arrive in Salem, the City of Peace, where we hope to live honestly and to die esteemed and regretted.

Leon Chautard.

---

37 Breed's Hill is where the Battle of Bunker Hill was actually fought in 1775.

Supplementary Readings

Frederick Douglass discusses the European revolutions of 1848

In the month of February of the present year, we may date the commencement of the great movements now progressing throughout Europe. In France, at that time, we saw a king to all appearance firmly seated on his costly throne, guarded by two hundred thousand bayonets. In the pride of his heart, he armed himself for the destruction of liberty. A few short hours ended the struggle. A shout went up to heaven from countless thousands, echoing back to earth, "Liberty—Equality—Fraternity." The troops heard the glorious sound, and fraternized with the people in the court yard of the Tuileries.—Instantly the King was but a man. All that was kingly fled. The throne whereon he sat was demolished; his splendid palace sacked; his royal carriage was burnt with fire; and he who had arrayed himself against freedom, found himself, like the great Egyptian tyrant, completely overwhelmed. Out of the ruins of this grand rupture, there came up a Republican Provisional Government, and snatching the revolutionary motto of "Liberty—Equality—Fraternity," from the fiery thousands who had just rolled back the tide of tyranny, they commenced to construct a State in accordance with that noble motto. Among the first of its acts, while hard pressed from without and perplexed within, beset on every hand—to the everlasting honor of that Government, it decreed the complete, unconditional emancipation of every slave throughout the French colonies. This act of justice and consistency went into effect on the 23d of last June. Thus were three hundred thousand souls admitted to the joys of freedom.—That provisional government is now no more. The brave and brilliant men who formed it, have ceased to play a conspicuous part in the political affairs of the nation. For the present, some of the brightest lights are obscured. Over the glory of the great-hearted Lamartine, the dark shadow of suspicion is cast.—The most of the members of that government are now distrusted, suspected, and slighted.—But while there remains on the earth one man of sable hue, there will be one witness who will ever remember with unceasing gratitude this noble act of that provisional government.

Sir, this act of justice to our race, on the part of the French people, has had a widespread effect upon the question of human freedom in our own land. Seldom, indeed, has the slave power of the nation received what they regarded such bad news. It placed our slaveholding Republic in a dilemma which all the world could see. We desired to rejoice with her in her republicanism, but it was impossible to do so without seeming to rejoice over abolitionism. Here inconsistency, hypocrisy, covered even the brass face of our slaveholding Republic with confusion. Even that staunch Democrat and Christian, John C. Calhoun, found himself embarrassed as to how to vote on a resolution congratulating the French people on the triumph of Republicanism over Royalty.

But to return to Europe. France is not alone the scene of commotion. Her excitable and inflammable disposition makes her an appropriate medium for lighting more substantial fires. Austria has dispensed with Metternich, while all the German States are demanding freedom; and even iron-hearted Russia is alarmed and perplexed by what is going on around her. The French metropolis is in direct communication with all the great cities of Europe, and the influence of her example is everywhere powerful. The Revolution of the 24th February has stirred the dormant energies of the oppressed classes all over the continent. Revolutions, outbreaks, and provisional governments, followed that event in almost fearful succession. A general insecurity broods over the crowned heads of Europe. Ireland, too, the land of O'Connell,[1] among the most powerful that ever advocated the cause of human freedom—Ireland, ever chafing under oppressive rule, famine-stricken, ragged and wretched, but warmhearted, generous and unconquerable Ireland, caught up the inspiring peal as it swept across the bosom of St. George's Channel, and again renewed her oath, to be free or die. Her cause is already sanctified by the martyrdom of Mitchell,[2] and millions stand ready to be sacrificed in the same manner. England, too—calm, dignified, brave old England—is not unmoved by what is going on through the sisterhood of European nations. Her toiling sons, from the buzz and din of the factory and workshop, to her endless coal mines deep down below the surface of the earth,

---

1 Daniel O'Connell was an Irish nationalist. Douglass met him in Dublin in 1845. A staunch critic of slavery, O'Connell was widely praised by U.S. abolitionists.

2 John Mitchel was an Irish nationalist who, in 1848, was sentenced to fourteen years' transportation. He was taken to Van Diemen's Land (Tasmania, Australia). He later made his way to the United States, where he published a paper attacking abolitionism and defending slavery.

have heard the joyful sound of "Liberty—Equality—Fraternity" and are lifting their heads and hearts in hope of better days.

These facts though unfortunately associated with great and crying evils—evils which you and I, and all of us must deeply deplore, are nevertheless interesting to the lovers of freedom and progress. They show that all sense of manhood and moral life, has not departed from the oppressed and plundered masses. They prove, that there yet remains an energy, when supported with the will that can roll back the combined and encroaching powers of tyranny and injustice. To teach this lesson, the movements abroad are important.

"First of August Celebration,"
The North Star, August 4, 1848.

Eugène Quesne and Claude Chambonnière deliver a lecture

On Friday evening, the lecture written by these gentlemen, and translated by Messrs. Jerome and Fabens, was read, at Lyceum Hall, by the Mayor. The audience was quite respectable, although not what it would have been, had the weather and the walking been more favorable.

Upon entering the hall, the Exiles were severally introduced to the company by the Mayor, who, before proceeding to read the lecture, gave an account of their personal history and circumstances, substantially as follows:

QUESNE is a lawyer by profession. As editor of a newspaper he incurred the displeasure of Louis Napoleon. He was roused from sleep one morning, in December, at the break of day, and found his bed surrounded by six armed men. He was instantly hurried off to an old prison, which had not for some years been tenanted on account of its insalubrity.—He was locked into a cold, damp, noisome cell, and left there, without food, fire, or a single article of furniture, of any kind whatever, for twenty-four hours. After that, the prisoners began to come in, and when 50 had been collected, they were carried, by night marches, to the coast, and transported to Cayenne.

CHAMBONNIERE was the teacher of a public school, and acted as Secretary of the Mayor of his city. Attempts were made to induce him to vote for Louis Napoleon. He refused any pledge, but declared that he should vote according to his convictions of duty. He did so. His ballot was secret. Upon suspicion that he had voted in the negative, he was turned out of employment, and the balance of salary due to him was forfeited. He remonstrated to the Minister of Public Instruction. His house was surrounded, at midnight, Dec. 26, 1851, by armed men, come to seize him. Having time only to put on his pantaloons, he barely escaped into the street, where he remained all night in a snow storm, without coat, or hat or shoes. Finding ultimate escape impossible, he was induced to deliver himself up. He was thrown into the cellar of a prison and kept there with 200 other men, for four months, their only food the most miserable and unpalatable apology for soup. Marched off, by night stages, to the coast, he also was transported to Cayenne.

They escaped from that place by paddling, at midnight, to an American vessel belonging to Salem, and secreting themselves in her. On her arrival at Surinam, the captain of a French ship of war demanded them of the American captain, but he peremptorily refused to deliver them up— claiming his right to protect them, as they had been mere political prisoners. The Governor of Surinam took the same ground—so did the American Consul there.—The fugitives were placed in a Gloucester vessel and arrived in safety at that port.

They are married men, with families, and are cut off from all communication, even by letter, with their friends in France. They are gentlemen of great propriety of demeanor, and by their manners, as well as their sufferings, have the strongest claims upon our sympathy and liberality.

The Mayor stated that the Irish patriot T. F. Meagher, took the deepest interest in these gentlemen, and left with him a liberal contribution to be added to the receipts of the lecture.

The lecture was written with great force and eloquence, and was duly appreciated by an intelligent and sympathizing audience.

At its conclusion QUESNE read a brief acknowledgment, in a simple and dignified style, in French.

> "The French Exiles,"
> *Salem Register*, February 7, 1853.

Louis Blanc pleads the cause of the French political prisoners in Cayenne

TO THE EDITOR OF THE TIMES.

Sir,—In February, 1855, I received a letter that was signed as follows:—"Tassilier, a political prisoner, transported in June, 1848, and who has now been working for 14 months, like many others among his fellow-sufferers, under a chain 40lb. in weight, with a cannon-ball at the end of it."

In that letter, dated "St. Joseph, Island of Despair, September, 1854," the gratuitous and unheard-of acts of barbarity were stated which are inflicted at Cayenne upon men belonging to all classes of society—artists, tradesmen, workmen, barristers, physicians, farmers, journalists, scholars—these men having been violently driven out of their country, not in consequence of any lawful judgment, but by the mere impulse of political passions. I was requested to lay before the civilized world the heartrending details, which I did as far as my power went.

Since that period no change whatever appears to have taken place in the situation of these unfortunate people, who are subjected to forced labour (*travaux forcés*) on a lonely rock, surrounded by the sea, at a distance of about 6,000 miles from their native land.

Six months ago a second letter was forwarded to me relating what follows:—

"Every ship that comes from the pestilential shores of Cayenne brings the death of a new victim. The latest victim is Peret, some time mayor of Beziers, a most generous-hearted man, feeling acutely, while he was rich, that many of his fellow-creatures were perishing of hunger, and ready to spare neither his fortune nor his life to the cause of humanity. Having been deported to Cayenne, without trial, for resisting the *coup d'état* of the 2d of December, he attempted, with six fellow-prisoners, to escape from that living tomb. They put to sea at night in a boat. Two hours after they were driven on the rocks. Peret, entangled in his cloak, was drowned. The six others survived. But what an existence! For two days they lived on what shellfish they could find on a desolate rock in the midst of the ocean, that threatened every moment to overwhelm them. At last one of them resolved to risk his life for the rest. Seeing no succour come, he threw himself into the sea, and, after three hours swimming, reached the land. Unhappily, the land was French Guiana. He could only save his life on condition of surrendering himself a prisoner. His five companions were rescued from the devouring sea only to be cast into another dungeon—tomb for tomb."

Now, Sir, here is a third letter which has just reached me:—

"To Mr. Louis Blanc those deported to Cayenne, with urgent request to make public this appeal:—

"Those deported to French Guiana make an appeal to the feelings of justice and humanity of all honest men, to whatever party they may belong.

"At the very moment when so much is spoken in France of clemency and generosity, while so many families are lulling themselves with the hope of clasping to their hearts the dear ones whose absence they have so long lamented, the political victims are treated in French Guiana in a manner worthy of the darkest ages of barbarity.

"It is certainly a painful task to unveil such an account of iniquity; but how is it possible to pass over in silence the unjust and cruel behaviour of French officers towards their fellow-countrymen? Let it be known, therefore, that we are unspeakably tortured on the flimsiest pretences, while people, deceived by the solemn declarations of the French Government, think perhaps that every prison is open and that we are at liberty. Let it be known, for instance, that out of five men lately arrested for some talk it had been the fancy of an overseer to invent, two were tied to a stake and dealt with as the most vile criminals. On their being reluctant to submit to an ignominious punishment soldiers were called for, who, rushing upon the victims, bruised them with blows, tore off their beards, and, reckless of shrieks with which wild beasts would have been moved, bound them with cords so fast as to make the blood gush.

"To relate all we suffer is more than we can possibly do. Our cheeks kindle with shame, and our hearts are bleeding. Suffice it to say that, while the French Government has its clemency cried up everywhere, there are Frenchmen in Guiana who do gasp for life. Nor are they allowed the so-journ of the Island of Despair, horrible as it is; barbarous administrators drag them violently on the continent, to compel them to a labour of eight hours a day in the marshy forests, from which pestilential vapours are continually rising.

"We refused to submit to this outrage upon laws, to this murderous attempt; we claimed promised liberty. The answer is 'death!'—a magnanimous answer, after the birth of a prince!

"Is there, indeed, for us any other prospect but imminent death? With no proper food, no garments, no shoes, no wine since February last, is there any chance that we should long be able to bear both the influence of an exhausting toil and a deadly climate? Again, where is the law which assimilates political proscripts to galley slaves? From beneath the brutal force that weighs upon us, heaped up together, almost breathless, but strengthened by the courage we draw from the sacredness of our cause and our hope in the triumph of justice, we protest against the violence which is offered to us. May public opinion be moved at our misfortunes, and energetically rise against deeds so well calculated to bring to shame a nation reputed the most enlightened and civilized in the world!

"BERBEJE ALEXANDRE	"DESSALLE
"GIBERT	"BIJOUX
"GORET	"DORE
"BOUDIN	"RAYMOND
"JECEGALY	"MEUNIERE
"DALIVIE	"CAYET
"FERNLAND	"CASNAC
"SOFFROIL	"FRISON
"PECH	"PATDOUANI
"GUERARD	"LABROUSSE
"BONNASSIOLLE	"AILHAUD
"SALLELES	"DAVAUX
"SUSINI	"BIVORS
"BEAUFOUR	"PERRIMOND
"LACOUR	"CHAUDRON
"BOCKENSKY	"PRIOL
"LAFOND	"CAUDRET
"DIME GUSTAVE	"CAUMETTE
"PELLETIER	"HOLLAS."

These are the lines, Sir, the insertion of which in your columns I earnestly request, not as a Republican—not even as a Frenchman—but as a man; for this is not a question of political feeling, it is one of simple justice and humanity. Let it be carefully remembered that the tortured victims are men who have never been tried by any lawful court, nor prosecuted by any form of law! It lies in your power, Sir—as I said on a similar occasion—that the groan they utter from the place where they are, so to speak, buried alive should be heard in the world of the living. The French press is gagged, and whoever has recently resided in France must of necessity know—as stated in a letter addressed by Mr. Aytoun to the most influential paper in this country—"that when the press is controlled by an arbitrary Government every species of injustice, jobbing, and oppression may be perpetrated, uncommented upon, and even unknown to the great majority of the population." Such being the case in France, the liberty of the English press remains the only possible resort for the oppressed to have the justice of their complaints at least examined. I apply, therefore, to the English press, and that all the more confidently since I read in *The Times* a few days ago:—"The press is emphatically the representative of the people. If wisely directed it guards the interests of all classes and conditions of society, and has a right in turn to the sympathies and assistance of all."

I remain, Sir, your most obedient servant,

LOUIS BLANC.

Aug. 23.

"The French Political Prisoners at Cayenne,"
Times (London), August 25, 1856.

Pierre Séroude tells his story in print

We departed from Demerara the twenty-ninth of October, upon a little three-master, called the *Amazon*, running to Baltimore (our fare paid by the English government); we arrived there the twenty-first of November, tired, worn out and wetted through. We were again in the same pecuniary embarrassment on reaching Baltimore, but the captain and the owner of the ship, gave us each a dollar, and put us on shore. The voyage on this ship was most uncomfortable for it was most always bad weather; we slept either on deck, or in the hold encumbered with hogsheads of molasses and sugar. The crew, as well as the captain, speaking no more french than we did english, could not understand our wants.

On leaving the ship, we went to sleep at the house of a negro, who gave us a comfortable supper, which moreover cost very little. This negro was the cook of our ship, and knowing nothing of us, and augering ill from our dress, was very hostile during the whole voyage; but on our arrival, he came to understand our unfortunate condition and endeavoured to make us forget, by many kindnesses, the ill treatment which he had caused us to undergo on board, and he succeeded.

Knowing no one in the city, by chance we fell into the hands of the French Society, to whom our thanks are due; they placed us in a boarding house where we were quite comfortable. We there met later, some friends dear to us, as they partook of our opinions, and whose sympathies were a great delight to us. The French Society sent us to embark upon a steamboat for Philadelphia, paying our passage and giving each of us half dollar, and the 24th of November in the evening we were on board. It was cold, and we asked if we could have some sheltered place; they said *no*, at first, but that on paying a half dollar we might be admitted into the Saloon. We paid this and so again found ourselves penniless.

At Philadelphia we were received by the correspondents of the French Society, who seemed to interest themselves in our condition, more than they had at Baltimore, and took a very generous course towards us for which we could only return our thanks. That evening they sent us by rail to the steamboat going to New-York, where we arrived the 26th of November 1856, and received the most friendly, the most distinguished, and the most lavish reception from our friends.

As for myself, I am living with Mr. L. Gros, in William Street, where I am the object of the most generous attention.

Pierre Séroude, *History of a Fugitive from Cayenne,*
Written by Himself (New York: French & American
Printing Office, 1857), 30–32.

William Lloyd Garrison and Helen Benson Garrison circulate *Escapes from Cayenne*

Boston, Feb. 6, 1858.

Dear Friend:

I have taken a very deep interest in the case of M. L. C. & his 2 companions, French refugees from the despotism of L[ouis] N[apoleon], who arrived at S[alem, Massachusetts] last summer, homeless, penniless, friendless, strangers in a strange land, among a people of strange speech. They are sufferers & martyrs in the cause of E[uropean] freedom—or, rather, freedom for all mankind, for they are ablst. in principle, & argue for the rights of the black man as they do for their own—as you will see, & be glad to see, on reading the thrilling N[arrative] of their escape from C[ayenne], written by Mr. C., & published in pamphlet form—25 copies of wh. I herewith send to your care, with the hope & belief that you will be able to dispose of them, as an act of charity, among your friends & acquaintance, at 25 cts. each. Mr. C. is an accomplished gent., & of a highly respectable family in France. He thought of going to your place to see whether he could find purchasers for his N[arrative]; but, his diffidence & foreign accent being hindrances to his success, I have feared that he would not be able to sell copies enough to cover his travelling expenses, & so I have undertaken to save him from all risk & uncertainty, by making up packages of 25 copies each, & sending them to reliable & kind-hearted friends, (as in your own case,) in various towns, asking their benevolent co-operation to this extent.

The N. is perfectly authentic, & highly recommended by some of the most respectable citizens in Salem, as you will see by referring to the printed cover of the pamphlet. Those who buy it will get their money's worth, & also do a most charitable deed; for two of these unfortunate men cannot speak a word of English—and as for employment in these "hard times," they cannot find any—so that they are in a state of complete destitution.

My wife, by exerting herself, has already succeeded in selling one hundred copies.

I know, my dear friend, you will not only excuse me for taking this liberty, but be glad to give your co-operation to this extent.

Yearning to see the day when the tyranny of Europe & the slavery of America shall be thoroughly "crushed out," I remain,

Yours, for universal freedom,
W. L. G.

> Letter from William Lloyd Garrison to an
> unknown correspondent, February 6, 1858,
> in *The Letters of William Lloyd Garrison*, vol. 4,
> *From Disunionism to the Brink of War, 1850–1860*,
> ed. Louis Ruchames (Cambridge, Mass.: Belknap Press
> of Harvard University Press, 1975), 510.

Léon Chautard defends socialism
and attacks slavery in *The Liberator*

The Boston *Journal* of March 25th contains an article entitled, "Socialists at a Sunday Banquet," in which foreign Republicans, and especially
the French Socialists, are denounced as infidels in religion, levellers in
politics, inveterate enemies of Christianity and social order, defying the
laws and public opinion. The *Journal* adds, "Their movements should be
watched by every true friend of well-regulated liberty"; and concludes as
follows:—"While we do not believe that this country will ever become de-
bauched by such levelling ideas, there is yet danger that the large class of
foreigners who hold these opinions, by a dexterous use of the balance of
power which they might possibly secure, may obtain a dangerous influence over party and the government."

We are called infidels in religion, because we meet on Sundays, and,
probably, because we do not believe that Joshua stopped the sun, and that
Samson killed a thousand Philistines, armed to the teeth, with the jaw-
bone of an ass. But if we, Frenchmen, meet on Sundays, it is because such
is the custom of our country, and of the whole of Europe, England ex-
cepted. We do not believe that Joshua stopped the sun, because the sun is
always still. (I could give many other good reasons, but I think the above
is sufficient.) We do not believe in the slaughter of the Philistines by Samson, in the manner described in the Bible, because we cannot suppose that
there is in the whole world a jaw strong enough,—not even Mr. Cushing's, one of the strongest,—to perform such a wonderful massacre without breaking into pieces.

But, with the exception of these three points, and some others of a trifling character, we are true believers in the Holy Bible. We believe that
all men come from Adam and Eve; then we believe that all mankind,—
white, red, yellow and black,—are *brothers*, and, as such, are born equally
free. From which it results that it is an outrageous crime, a shameful, in-
excusable robbery, to deprive anyone of his liberty, of the possession of
himself. We believe that a man, made a slave, against the laws of nature,
justice and humanity, has a right to reconquer by force his stolen property, his freedom. The United States exercised this right in their struggle against England, Frenchmen assisted them, and the whole world applauded the proclamation of independence. The companions of Lafayette

and Rochambeau were the ancestors of those so cowardly insulted by the Boston *Journal*. Do not forget it, Americans!

In consequence of the above principle, a slave has a right to kill the master, who, by force, keeps him in bondage. Then Orsini and his companions had a right to kill Louis Napoleon Bonaparte, who had sent an army to enslave their native country.

If the editor of the *Journal* believes there is but one race of men, he is quite wrong to be pro-slavery. If he thinks there are several races of men, he does not believe the Bible, and he is wrong to call us infidels in religion. He is more infidel than we,—he is quite an infidel.

As an American, the editor of the *Journal* has a right to say that the Bible was not made for him, as the holy book says nothing about America and Americans. Both were unknown when it was written.

The *Journal* confesses that tyranny and poverty are casting upon the shores of the United States Germans and Frenchmen, whose principles are subversive of social order, &c. &c. It is impossible to be more illogical; the first part of the sentence is the condemnation of the second. If tyranny obliges us to leave our country, we are right in trying, by all means, to break tyranny. If we are so poor in our country, and you are so rich in America, is it because we are less industrious or less fond of work than you are? Certainly not; the editor of the *Journal* knows the contrary. Is it because Germany and France are less fertile than the United States? Evidently not; they produce abundantly every thing. Every one knows that France could amply supply with all the necessaries of life, a population ten times more numerous than hers,—that is to say, the population of the whole world. This has been proved by Raspail and other eminent men.

What is the reason, then, why German and French laborers are so poor? It is only because the social institutions of those countries are wrong; it is because they grant the greatest part of the produce to idle men, and nothing to the laborer. Consequently, the Socialists, or *reformers of social institutions*, are very right and true. Their principles are not subversive of social order, but, on the contrary, the social order now existing in France and Germany is subversive of right, justice and equity.

We do not know what the *Journal* calls a "well-regulated liberty." Is it the liberty preached by Mr. Caleb Cushing, practised by Gen. Walker, and ruled by Mr. Buchanan? We call such a liberty a perfectly well regulated slavery of four millions of human beings, by a perfectly dishonest association of three hundred thousand ruffians, liars and thieves.

We are called "levellers"; but we are proud of this title. Yes, we are "levellers," and we are so because we sincerely think that, in modern societies, the social mountains are too high, and the social abysses are too deep. We will cut off the barren and frozen summits of the mountains, and with them we will fill up the dark and desolate abysses, on purpose to transform the former into pleasant hills, and the latter into joyful valleys.

The *Journal* says we are dangerous to the country. If it really thinks so, the best it can do is to beg of His Excellency, President Buchanan, and of the Senate and House, to pass a bill similar to the English Conspirators' Bill.[3] Perhaps the motion will be agreed to, after the Constitution shall be imposed (if possible) on the free people of Kansas.

But, in that case, we honestly fear this: the Lecompton Constitution[4] can be the end of the beginning, and the Conspirators' Bill could be the beginning of the end. Amen.

LEON CHAUTARD, a French Socialist.
Salem, Mass., March 27, 1858.

"Conspirators' Bill in the United States,"
The Liberator, April 16, 1858.

3 The Conspiracy to Murder Bill of 1858 was introduced by the British government following Felice Orsini's attempted assassination of Napoleon III (the attack had been planned in Britain). The bill made conspiracy to murder a felony and clarified that the law covered conspiracies to commit offenses abroad as well as in Britain. It was rejected, leading to the prime minister's resignation.

4 The Lecompton Constitution was one of four proposed constitutions for the state of Kansas. It was drawn up in 1857 by proslavery advocates of Kansas statehood and received the support of the Democratic president James Buchanan. The constitution was ultimately rejected, and Kansas entered the Union as a free state in 1861.

SUGGESTIONS FOR FURTHER READING

Anderson, Clare. *Convicts: A Global History*. Cambridge: Cambridge University Press, 2022.

Baptist, Edward E. *The Half Has Never Been Told: Slavery and the Making of American Capitalism*. New York: Basic Books, 2014.

Beecher, Jonathan. *Victor Considerant and the Rise of French Romantic Socialism*. Berkeley: University of California Press, 2001.

——. *Writers and Revolution: Intellectuals and the French Revolution of 1848*. Cambridge: Cambridge University Press, 2021.

Blumenthal, Henry. *American and French Culture, 1800–1900: Interchanges in Art, Science, Literature, and Society*. Baton Rouge: Louisiana State University Press, 1975.

Chamoiseau, Patrick. *French Guiana: Memory Traces of the Penal Colony*. Translated by Matt Reeck. Middletown, Conn.: Wesleyan University Press, 2020.

Clark, Christopher. *Revolutionary Spring: Europe Aflame and the Fight for a New World, 1848–1849*. New York: Crown, 2023.

Corcoran, Paul E., ed. *Before Marx: Socialism and Communism in France, 1830–48*. London: Macmillan, 1983.

Curti, Merle. "The Impact of the Revolutions of 1848 on American Thought." *Proceedings of the American Philosophical Society* 93, no. 3 (1949): 209–15.

Curtis, Sarah A. "Missionary Utopias: Anne-Marie Javouhey and the Colony at Mana, French Guiana, 1827–1848." In *View from the Margins: Creating Identities in Modern France*, edited by Kevin J. Callahan and Sarah A. Curtis, 21–52. Lincoln: University of Nebraska Press, 2008.

Davis, Stacey Renee. "Turning French Convicts into Colonists: The Second Empire's Political Prisoners in Algeria, 1852–1858." *French Colonial History* 2 (2002): 93–113.

Delnore, Allyson Jaye. "Empire by Example? Deportees in France and Algeria and the Re-Making of a Modern Empire, 1846–1854." *French Politics, Culture & Society* 33, no. 1 (2015): 33–54.

———. "Political Convictions: French Deportation Projects in the Age of Revolutions, 1791–1854." PhD diss., University of Virginia, 2004.

Doyle, Don H. *The Cause of All Nations: An International History of the American Civil War.* New York: Basic Books, 2015.

Eichhorn, Niels. *Atlantic History in the Nineteenth Century: Migration, Trade, Conflict, and Ideas.* Cham, Switzerland: Palgrave Macmillan, 2019.

Evans, R. J. W., and Hartmut Pogge von Strandmann, eds. *The Revolutions in Europe, 1848–1849: From Reform to Reaction.* Oxford: Oxford University Press, 2000.

Fabian, Ann. *The Unvarnished Truth: Personal Narratives in Nineteenth-Century America.* Berkeley: University of California Press, 2000.

Fagan, Benjamin. "*The North Star* and the Atlantic 1848." *African American Review* 47, no. 1 (2014): 51–67.

Fleche, Andre M. *The Revolution of 1861: The American Civil War in the Age of Nationalist Conflict.* Chapel Hill: University of North Carolina Press, 2012.

Foster, Frances Smith. *Witnessing Slavery: The Development of Ante-bellum Slave Narratives.* 2nd ed. Madison: University of Wisconsin Press, 1994.

Gleeson, David T., and Simon Lewis, eds. *The Civil War as Global Conflict: Transnational Meanings of the American Civil War.* Columbia: University of South Carolina Press, 2014.

Griffin, Sean. "Antislavery Utopias: Communitarian Labor Reform and the Abolitionist Movement." *Journal of the Civil War Era* 8, no. 2 (2018): 243–68.

Guarneri, Carl J. *The Utopian Alternative: Fourierism in Nineteenth-Century America.* Ithaca, N. Y.: Cornell University Press, 1991.

Hartman, Janine C. "Transatlantic Spartacus." In *The Afterlife of John Brown,* edited by Andrew Taylor and Eldrid Herrington, 145–58. New York: Palgrave Macmillan, 2005.

Helg, Aline. *Slave No More: Self-Liberation before Abolitionism in the Americas.* Chapel Hill: University of North Carolina Press, 2019.

Honeck, Mischa. "'Freemen of All Nations, Bestir Yourselves': Felice Orsini's Transnational Afterlife and the Radicalization of America." *Journal of the Early Republic* 30, no. 4 (2010): 587–615.

———. *We Are the Revolutionists: German-Speaking Immigrants and American Abolitionists after 1848.* Athens: University of Georgia Press, 2011.

Jackson, Holly. *American Radicals: How Nineteenth-Century Protest Shaped the Nation.* New York: Crown, 2019.

Jackson, Kellie Carter. *Force and Freedom: Black Abolitionists and the Politics of Violence.* Philadelphia: University of Pennsylvania Press, 2019.

Jennings, Lawrence C. *French Anti-Slavery: The Movement for the Abolition of Slavery in France, 1802–1848.* Cambridge: Cambridge University Press, 2000.

Kachun, Mitch. "'Our Platform Is as Broad as Humanity': Transatlantic Freedom

Movements and the Idea of Progress in Nineteenth-Century African American Thought and Activism." *Slavery & Abolition* 24, no. 3 (2003): 1–23.

Kloos, Peter. *The Maroni River Caribs of Surinam.* Assen, Netherlands: Van Gorcum, 1971.

Marrs, Cody. "Frederick Douglass in 1848." *American Literature* 85, no. 3 (2013): 447–73.

McDaniel, W. Caleb. *The Problem of Democracy in the Age of Slavery: Garrisonian Abolitionists and Transatlantic Reform.* Baton Rouge: Louisiana State University Press, 2013.

Moggach, Douglas, and Gareth Stedman Jones, eds. *The 1848 Revolutions and European Political Thought.* Cambridge: Cambridge University Press, 2018.

Morrison, Michael A. "American Reaction to European Revolutions, 1848–1852: Sectionalism, Memory, and the Revolutionary Heritage." *Civil War History* 49, no. 2 (2003): 111–32.

Oldfield, J. R. *The Ties that Bind: Transatlantic Abolitionism in the Age of Reform, c. 1820–1865.* Liverpool: Liverpool University Press, 2020.

Olsavsky, Jesse. *The Most Absolute Abolition: Runaways, Vigilance Committees, and the Rise of Revolutionary Abolitionism, 1835–1861.* Baton Rouge: Louisiana State University Press, 2022.

Price, Richard, ed. *Maroon Societies: Rebel Slave Communities in the Americas.* 3rd ed. Baltimore: Johns Hopkins University Press, 1996.

———, and Sally Price. *Maroons in Guyane: Past, Present, Future.* Athens: University of Georgia Press, 2022.

Rapport, Mike. *1848: Year of Revolution.* New York: Basic Books, 2010.

Reynolds, Larry J. *European Revolutions and the American Literary Renaissance.* New Haven, Conn.: Yale University Press, 1988.

Roberts, Timothy Mason. *Distant Revolutions: 1848 and the Challenge to American Exceptionalism.* Charlottesville: University of Virginia Press, 2009.

Rohrs, Richard C. "American Critics of the French Revolution of 1848." *Journal of the Early Republic* 14, no. 3 (1994): 359–77.

Roy, Michaël. *Fugitive Texts: Slave Narratives in Antebellum Print Culture.* Translated by Susan Pickford. Madison: University of Wisconsin Press, 2022.

———. "'Throwing Pearls Before Swine': The Strange Publication History of *Vie de Frédéric Douglass, esclave américain* (1848)." *Slavery & Abolition* 40, no. 4 (2019): 727–49.

Sainlaude, Stève. *France and the American Civil War: A Diplomatic History.* Translated by Jessica Edwards. Chapel Hill: University of North Carolina Press, 2019.

Sanchez, Jean-Lucien. "The French Empire, 1542–1976." In *A Global History of Convicts and Penal Colonies,* edited by Clare Anderson, 123–56. London: Bloomsbury, 2018.

Sinha, Manisha. *The Slave's Cause: A History of Abolition.* New Haven, Conn.: Yale University Press, 2016.

Sperber, Jonathan. *The European Revolutions, 1848–1851*. 2nd ed. Cambridge: Cambridge University Press, 2005.

Thompson, Alvin O. *Flight to Freedom: African Runaways and Maroons in the Americas*. Kingston, Jamaica: University of the West Indies Press, 2006.

Traugott, Mark. *Armies of the Poor: Determinants of Working-Class Participation in the Parisian Insurrection of June 1848*. Princeton, N.J.: Princeton University Press, 1985.

Tuchinsky, Adam-Max. "'The Bourgeoisie Will Fall and Fall Forever': The *New-York Tribune*, the 1848 French Revolution, and American Social Democratic Discourse." *Journal of American History* 92, no. 2 (2005): 470–97.

Weyler, Karen A. *Empowering Words: Outsiders and Authorship in Early America*. Athens: University of Georgia Press, 2013.

RACE IN THE ATLANTIC WORLD, 1700–1900

The Hanging of Angélique:
The Untold Story of Canadian Slavery
and the Burning of Old Montréal
BY AFUA COOPER

Christian Ritual and the Creation of
British Slave Societies, 1650–1780
BY NICHOLAS M. BEASLEY

African American Life in the Georgia Lowcountry:
The Atlantic World and the Gullah Geechee
EDITED BY PHILIP MORGAN

The Horrible Gift of Freedom: Atlantic Slavery and
the Representation of Emancipation
BY MARCUS WOOD

The Life and Letters of Philip Quaque,
the First African Anglican Missionary
EDITED BY VINCENT CARRETTA
AND TY M. REESE

In Search of Brightest Africa:
Reimagining the Dark Continent in
American Culture, 1884–1936
BY JEANNETTE EILEEN JONES

Contentious Liberties:
American Abolitionists in
Post-Emancipation Jamaica, 1834–1866
BY GALE L. KENNY

We Are the Revolutionists:
German-Speaking Immigrants and
American Abolitionists after 1848
BY MISCHA HONECK

The American Dreams of John B. Prentis, Slave Trader
BY KARI J. WINTER

Missing Links: The African and American Worlds
of R. L. Garner, Primate Collector
BY JEREMY RICH

Almost Free: A Story about Family and
Race in Antebellum Virginia
BY EVA SHEPPARD WOLF

Printed in the United States
by Baker & Taylor Publisher Services